necklaces

by Tansy Wilson

THE GUILD OF MASTER CRAFTSMAN
PUBLICATIONS

Guild of
Master Craftsman
Publications

First published 2012 by
Guild of Master Craftsman Publications Ltd
Castle Place, 166 High Street, Lewes,
East Sussex BN7 1XU

Text and illustrations © Tansy Wilson, 2012
Copyright in the Work © GMC Publications Ltd, 2012

ISBN 978 1 86108 864 2

Set in King and Myriad
Colour origination by GMC Reprographics
Printed and bound by Hung Hing
Printing Co. Ltd in China

Publisher Jonathan Bailey
Production Manager Jim Bulley
Managing Editor Gerrie Purcell
Senior Project Editor Dominique Page
Editor Sarah Hoggett
Managing Art Editor Gilda Pacitti
Photographer Andrew Perris
Designer Simon Goggin

Please renew or return items by the date shown on your receipt

www.hertsdirect.org/libraries

Renewals and enquiries: 0300 123 4049

Textphone for hearing or speech impaired   0300 123 4041

Hertfordshi

contents

Tools and equipment

Materials and Findings

Techniques

Continued...

HONEYBEE

LA MER

RAINBOW

The Projects

MILITARY

KNOTTY

SONGBIRD

SCOUBIDOU

CAMEO

STELLA

AUDREY

HARVEST

BUTTERFLY

TWISTS

ILLUSION

WEAVER

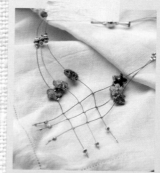

CRISS-CROSS

VINTAGE

ZIPPY

CIRCLES

ROCKER

Tools and equipment

THE FOLLOWING PAGES LIST AND EXPLAIN SOME
OF THE MOST COMMONLY USED TOOLS YOU WILL
NEED TO MAKE YOUR NECKLACES.

pliers

When holding, forming or shaping pieces of jewellery, the most common tools used are pliers. You can get different types that are designed for particular uses. However, even if you have just one pair of multi pliers, you should be able to tackle most jobs.

ROUND-NOSE PLIERS

These pliers have round, tapered jaws that start small at the very tip and increase to a larger circumference at the base. They are used for making eye pins, wrapping loops and shaping wire.

FLAT-NOSE PLIERS

These pliers have flat parallel jaws at the top and bottom. They are handy for bending sharp corners or straightening wire, crimping flat ribbon crimps and holding, opening and closing jump rings and other small components.

SNIPE-NOSE PLIERS

Sometimes known as chain-nose pliers, these pliers have half-round jaws with flat parallel inside faces that touch. They are also tapered from small at the very tip of the nose to a larger half-round at the base. Their unique shape makes them ideal for holding small jewellery components, opening and closing chain links or jump rings and shaping wire in general.

CRIMPING PLIERS

Crimping pliers come in a variety of sizes and it is important to have the correct size jaw for the crimps that you most commonly use. The jaw has two sections: the back forms your crimp tube into a curve, trapping the contents; and the front folds the crimp in half, securing everything in place.

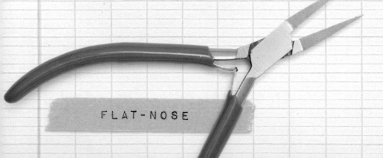

FLAT-NOSE

MULTI PLIERS

This pair of pliers combines the functions of both the flat-nose pliers and the round-nose pliers, as the jaws change shape halfway down. They even have a cutting surface on them, too, making them an ideal pair of pliers for first-time jewellery makers.

MULTI-SIZED LOOPING PLIERS /WIRE WRAP MANDRELS

With many sizes of round jaws on one surface, multi-sized looping pliers enable you to make jump rings and loops to a certain size. Wire wrap mandrels are a less expensive option of exactly the same tool.

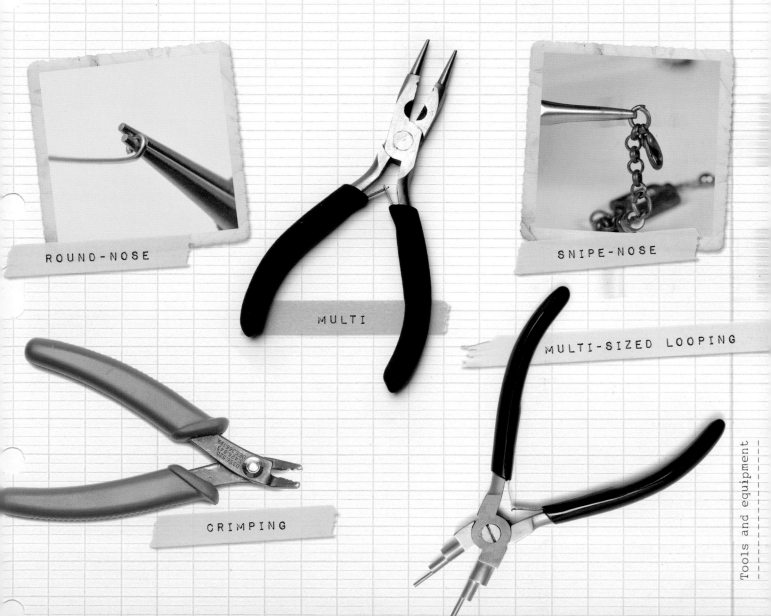

ROUND-NOSE

SNIPE-NOSE

MULTI

MULTI-SIZED LOOPING

CRIMPING

cutters

There are various types and sizes of cutters used in jewellery making. To simplify their uses: top and side cutters are used for cutting thin materials and wire; snips for cutting sheet material; and scissors for cutting paper and fabric.

TOP CUTTERS

The actual cutting surface on this tool is at the very top, as the name suggests. Materials such as wire can be cut at 90 degrees, extremely close and flush to your piece.

SIDE CUTTERS

These work in a very similar way to top cutters; this time, however, the cutting surface is on the side of the tool. The nose is also slightly tapered, enabling you to gain access to smaller areas in your piece.

SNIPS

Snips are often seen as a pair of scissors for sheet metal, but they are also useful for trimming ribbon or leather. Be aware, though, that they will leave a mark on the surface when cutting.

SCISSORS

General-purpose scissors should have a fine, long nose so that you can reach into small areas, and be sharp so that you can accurately cut fabric and paper.

PIERCING SAW AND BLADES

This tool uses separate saw blades for cutting wire, tube and sheet metal. It gives an extremely clean cut without marking the surface at all. Piercing saws are ideal for making jump rings, as they cut the wire completely flush without leaving an indent. This ensures that the jump rings close nice and tightly.

PIERCING SAW AND BLADES

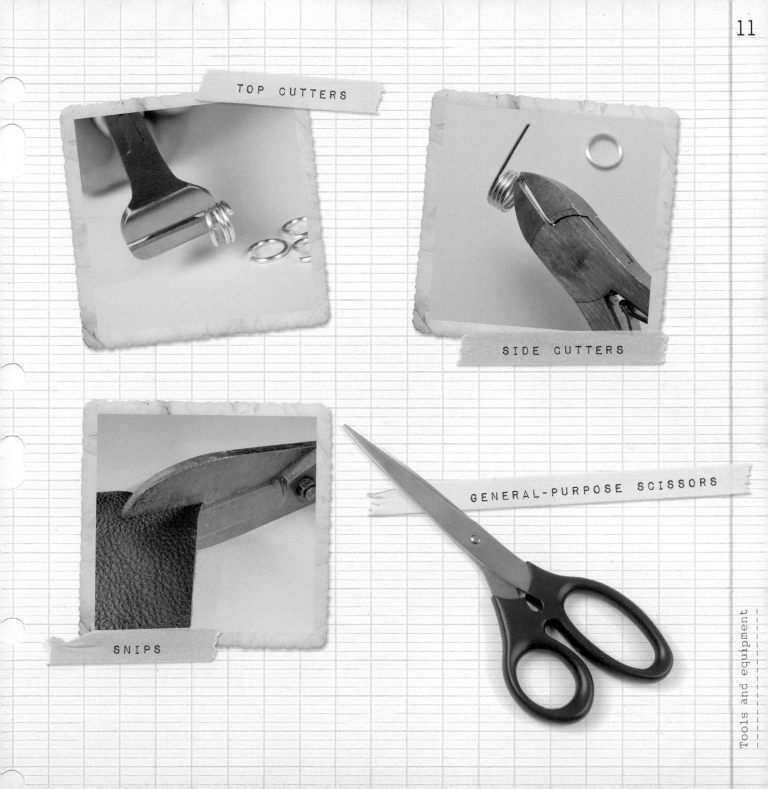

TOP CUTTERS

SIDE CUTTERS

SNIPS

GENERAL-PURPOSE SCISSORS

miscellaneous tools

The following section looks at some of the basics
that are essential for any jewellery tool box.

BRADAWL

With its very sharp point, a bradawl enables you to
pierce a hole in various plastics and fabrics. It is not
recommended for sheet metal or wire.

BEAD BOARD

This is a great tool for planning the length of your
necklaces. The channels have measurements on them;
by placing your beads in the channels, you can see
exactly how many you will require. The compartments
in the middle are for holding the findings that you will
be using for that particular piece.

BEAD MAT

A less expensive equivalent of the bead board, this
cushioned, soft mat stops your beads and findings from
rolling around. It does not have any compartments in it.

BEADING NEEDLE

A beading needle is made from extremely fine wire
formed into a needle shape. What makes it special
is that the 'eye' collapses, enabling you to string even
the smallest of beads with ease.

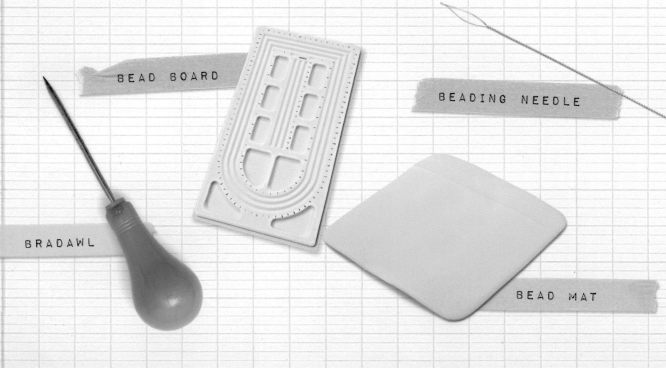

BEAD BOARD

BEADING NEEDLE

BRADAWL

BEAD MAT

SEWING NEEDLE AND THREAD

SEWING NEEDLES AND THREAD

Some of the projects require you to sew components in place. It is always a good idea to have a range of needles and different-coloured cotton threads for various craft projects.

ADHESIVE

A quick-setting adhesive (Cyanoacrylate) is ideal for use on all types of beads and threads. Adding a drop onto knots provides extra security. There are also two-part adhesives, which you mix together to form a thicker-consistency adhesive. These are useful where you do not want glue to run onto other surfaces.

TAPE MEASURE

Whether you're working with wire or fabric, a tape measure is essential for measuring your materials to obtain accurate lengths for your design.

SHAPE CUTTERS

Rather than using scissors to cut out your design, you can buy ready-made cutters that enable you to 'stamp' out an exact shape over and over again. There is even a machine available that can cut and texture a wide range of materials all at the same time.

TWO-PART ADHESIVE

SHAPE CUTTER

ADHESIVE

TAPE MEASURE

Materials and findings

THE FOLLOWING SECTION LOOKS AT A VARIETY OF MATERIALS AVAILABLE, FROM BEADS TO THE STRINGING MATERIALS AND FINDINGS MOST COMMONLY USED TO CREATE FABULOUS NECKLACES.

beads and charms

There is such a massive variety of beads and charms available that it can be daunting to know which ones to buy. Start with your favourite colours and shapes and just keep adding to your collection. It's also a good idea to have a theme, so that you can collect beads, charms, ribbons and even fabrics to match that style.

recycled pieces

You do not always have to buy new. You can recycle broken bits of
jewellery or buttons from unworn clothes. Charity shops and jumble
sales are often a good source of unique pieces at bargain prices.
Even everyday items such as safety pins, zips and packaging can
be turned into beautiful designs.

stringing materials

When making your necklaces, you will at some point need to make
a decision on the most suitable stringing material for your design.
Here are some of the materials available and their key characteristics.

ELASTIC

Elastic comes in many varieties. There are thread-covered elastics (more commonly used in sewing) and also multi-strand elastics, both of which are excellent for tying knots in, as the way they are made means the elastic is not slippery. They are, however, easier to snap, so you may need to use extra lengths for doubling up when stringing.

The other variety of elastic is extremely durable, shiny and transparent. Being transparent, it is often used where you do not want the stringing material to interfere visually with the design; this is often referred to as illusion elastic. However, its surface is slippery and therefore is best crimped rather than knotted, although you can add a drop of glue to any knots.

NYLON

This thread is like a fishing line in that it is extremely strong. It comes in many sizes, starting from threads as thin as a hair. Its fineness related to its strength makes it extremely versatile in most stringing projects. It is also easy to tie knots in – but again, I would advise adding a drop of glue to secure them.

NYLON-COATED WIRE

Often referred to as 'TigerTail', this is constructed of several fine steel wires bound together in a nylon coating. It is stronger than nylon, but cannot be successfully knotted; ideally, you should use crimps to add any fixings. As it comes in a variety of thicknesses and colours, you can often make this form of stringing a feature of your design.

NYLON

ELASTIC

NYLON-COATED WIRE

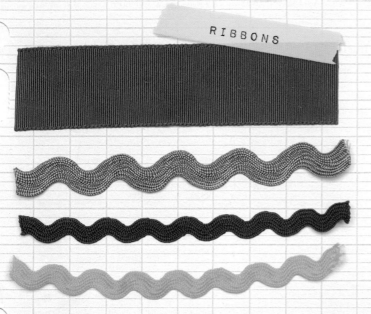

RIBBONS

CHAIN

CHAIN

Although this seems an obvious category, I have included it to highlight the fact that there are so many styles of chain in a wide variety of sizes and colours that the chain can really become a feature of your design in its own right, rather than just something to add a pendant onto.

SUEDE AND LEATHER THONG

If you are using real suede or leather, you may be restricted to length; however, there are lots of synthetic equivalents in a wide range of sizes and colours, making this material a tactile feature to consider in your designs.

RIBBONS

Ribbons come in an enormous variety of sizes, shapes, patterns and colours, making them ideal to use when you want to add an immediate vibe to your design. You can simply tie bows on or incorporate them as the main method of joining by using ribbon crimps.

SUEDE AND LEATHER THONG

clasps

There are so many different types of clasp available that I have given them their own category to identify each of their main characteristics. In your necklaces, you may want to make a feature of a clasp or simply choose one that is easy to use.

BOLT RING

This is a round ring that has a spring-loaded trigger to open up part of the ring. They come in all different sizes.

CARIBINER

More commonly known as a lobster, trigger or parrot clasp, this is much like the bolt ring in that there is a trigger to open up part of the clasp. The overall shape, however, is not round but elongated, so you can get a much better grip on it. Again, they come in all different sizes.

MAGNETIC

This is the easiest clasp of all to open and close. There are no little triggers to find: it just simply works on natural magnetic pole forces keeping the two ends together.

TOGGLE

This clasp consists of an open shape that is attached to one end of your necklace and a toggle bar that's connected to the other end. To close the clasp, just slide the toggle bar through the open shape. The variety of designs and sizes available means that this clasp will make a real feature on any necklace.

FANCY

This is a general term I have used for any other style of clasp. They can be heavily decorated or recycled from vintage pieces (see the Audrey Project on page 70). Using a fancy clasp can add that designer touch to any necklace.

other findings

Findings is a word given to all the little bits and pieces used in jewellery making that are not beads or charms. (Clasps are findings, too, but they are such an important part of making necklaces, that I've put them in a category of their own.) There is a huge choice available to buy. On the following pages are the ones I have used regularly throughout this book.

BEAD CUPS

Bead cups are small metal cup shapes that fit over the top or bottom of a bead. They add a decorative element to a design.

CALOTTES

Before use, calottes look like open clam shells with a hook attached. They have a small hole through which you pass your stringing material before knotting or crimping it so that it cannot pass back through the hole; you then close the two halves to conceal the knot.

CHAIN ENDS

As the name suggests, chain ends are basically tubes into which you glue or squash chain or other stringing materials to neatly finish the ends of your necklaces.

CONNECTORS

This is a general term for a shape that has a loop at each end so you can connect it easily to other findings. Connectors come in lots of shapes and sizes and are definitely a feature for any design.

CRIMP TUBES AND COVERS

This is a more elaborate version of a calotte, consisting of a little tube that you crimp using crimping pliers (see page 22) and a cover that you wrap over it to finish it off.

EXTENDER CHAINS

These are often 2-in (50mm) lengths of chain that you can add to the end of a necklace, giving the wearer the opportunity to wear the same piece of jewellery at two different lengths.

HEAD PINS AND EYE PINS

These are metal wires with a pin head or an eye loop at one end. They are very useful for threading and connecting beads together.

CONNECTORS

EXTENDER CHAINS

HEAD PINS

CRIMP TUBES AND COVERS

EYE PINS

JUMP RINGS

A jump ring is a single ring of metal that is mainly used to join or link pieces together. You close the ring to secure the item in place.

NOODLE TUBES

These are tubes that come in a variety of sizes and straight or curved shapes to allow stringing material to pass through them, creating decorative spaces between beads.

RIBBON CRIMPS

These little metal crimps are used for neatly fastening the ends of materials such as ribbon, leather, suede and cords. They often have a loop attached, so that you can easily connect them to other findings.

WIRE CHOKERS

An alternative to stringing materials, a wire choker is a stiff wire which you can thread or wire beads onto.

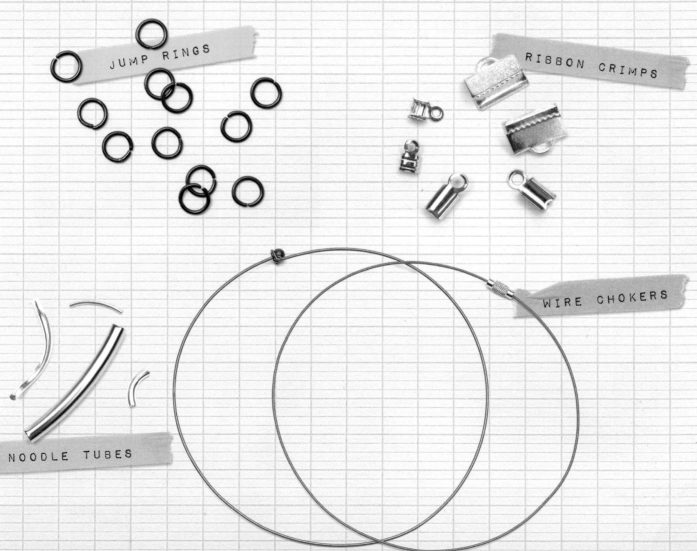

JUMP RINGS

RIBBON CRIMPS

WIRE CHOKERS

NOODLE TUBES

Techniques

THE FOLLOWING PAGES ILLUSTRATE SOME OF THE BASIC TECHNIQUES AND TIPS YOU WILL NEED WHEN YOU START TO MAKE YOUR OWN NECKLACES.

crimps and calottes

Crimps and calottes are used to join stringing materials such as illusion elastic or nylon-coated wire to findings and clasps in places where knots cannot be used. They are an extremely secure and professional-looking fastening.

USING CRIMPING PLIERS

1 Thread a crimp tube onto your stringing material, then pass the thread through the finding and back through the crimp tube. Slide the tube along so that it is close to the finding.

2 Hold the crimp tube in the crescent-shaped section of the crimping pliers and squash the crimp tube into a curved shape.

3 Finish the crimping process by moving the now curved crimp tube to the front circular section of the crimping pliers, folding the crimp in half.

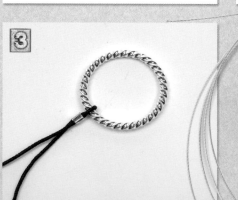

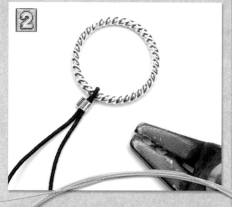

USING CALOTTES

1   Thread the end of your stringing
    material through the hole in the
    centre of the calotte.

2   Either slide a crimp tube over
    the end of the stringing material
    and crimp it or tie a knot or two
    so that the stringing material
    cannot pass back through the
    hole. Add a drop of glue if you
    are using slippery material.

3   Slide the calotte up to the crimp
    or knot and, using flat-nose
    pliers, gently squeeze the two
    hemispheres together so that
    they close over the crimp or knot.

4   The calotte has a little tail of wire.
    This can be formed into an eye
    loop so that it can be attached
    to other findings. Cut away any
    excess thread that is not required.

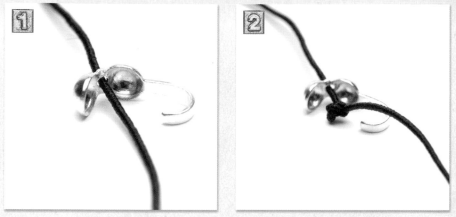

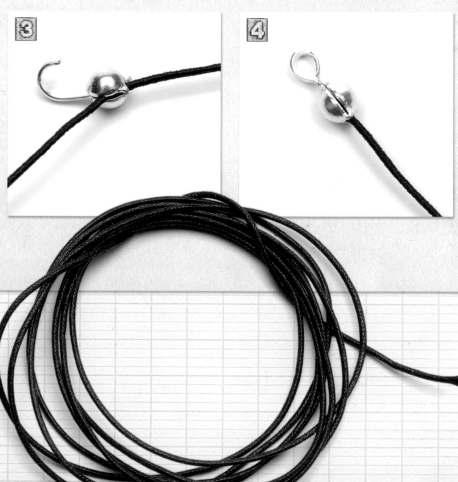

ribbon crimps and chain ends

Both ribbon crimps and chain ends are findings that are used to fasten the ends of ribbons, cord or chain neatly to other findings.

USING RIBBON CRIMPS

1 Place the end of your fabric, ribbon or cord in the jaws of the ribbon crimp. Some crimps have jagged teeth to help catch the fibres and prevent it from pulling out.

2 Using flat-nose pliers, gently squash the jaws of the crimp together, trapping the contents. Some jaws fold over one another, but the principle of squashing the jaws over the ribbon is the same.

USING CHAIN ENDS

1 Place your chain or cord in the tube section of the chain end.

2 Depending upon the style of the chain end, either glue them in place or, using snipe-nose pliers, squash the middle section of the tube, trapping the contents. With either approach, adding glue gives extra security.

jump rings

A jump ring is a single ring of metal that is most commonly used to join or link pieces together.

OPENING AND CLOSING JUMP RINGS

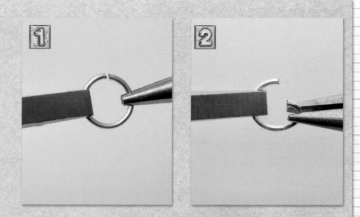

1 Hold a jump ring between two pairs of pliers, each with a flat parallel nose, so that the opening of the jump ring is at the top.

2 Twist the pliers in your left hand away from your body and the pliers in your right hand towards your body. This will open the jump ring without losing the shape of the circle. Twist back to close. Ensure both the metal edges of the ring click together as you close them.

MAKING JUMP RINGS

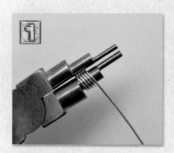

1 Coil a length of round wire tightly around a wire wrap mandrel or multi-sized looping pliers. If you do not have either of these tools, wrap the wire around a cylindrical shape such as a pen or lipstick case (depending on the size of jump ring required). The number of coils made will determine the number of jump rings you will make.

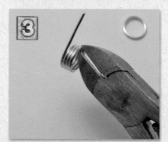

2 Slide the coil of wire up until one loop of wire comes off the tool or cylindrical object and using a piercing saw to create a straight edge, cut through the first coil. Repeat the process, cutting off one ring at a time.

3 Alternatively, use side or top cutters to cut the rings off one at a time.

eye and head pins

A head pin is a length of wire with a pin head at one end, allowing you to thread beads onto the wire without them falling off. An eye pin is also a length of wire but it has a loop at one end so you can join components onto it.

open eye loops

An open eye loop is a loop that you make as close to the top of a bead as possible. This loop will allow you to link your bead onto other components or chain.

MAKING EYE PINS

1 Using round-nose pliers, hold a piece of wire at the very end. The length of wire you use is determined by the size and number of beads that you want to thread on it, while the size of the eye hole is determined by how far up the nose of the pliers you grip the wire.

2 Twist the pliers to form a small closed loop.

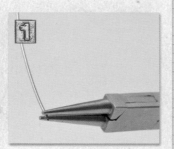

3 Move this loop in your pliers so the long end can be pushed against the other round-nose jaw to centre the eye pin loop over the long length of wire.

OPEN EYE LOOPS AT THE TOP OF A BEAD

1 Thread a head pin through your chosen bead and bend the long length of the head pin back against the bead.

2 Using round-nose pliers, grip the wire at the very top of the bead. Holding the long end of the wire, wrap this all the way around the nose of the pliers until the wire crosses and meets itself. Cut the excess wire away at this point using side or top cutters.

closed loops

Closed loops are the most secure method of attaching beads. They are very similar to open eye loops, except that once you have wired your chosen bead on to your design, the only way to remove it is to physically cut it off.

WIRING ON A BEAD USING A CLOSED LOOP

1 Thread a head pin through your chosen bead and bend the long length of the head pin back against the bead.

2 Using round nose pliers, grip the wire at the very top of the bead. Bend the long length of the head pin around the nose of the pliers until it nearly meets itself where you are holding it in your pliers; it should form a hook shape.

3 Next, thread the wire onto a component such as a length of chain, so that it hangs down from the hook you created in step 2.

4 Hold the top of the hook in snipe nose pliers and hold the tip of the long end in your other hand. Start to wrap this long end around the base of the hook, spiralling the wire around itself. Cut off any excess wire.

chains and wires

honeybee

Finding these wonderful bee charms provided me with the inspiration to create a busy statement necklace of gold and black beads.

Everything you will need...

Adding lots of beads to one chain makes a decadent, clustered statement. With this technique it's all about the beads: using different shapes and colours to the ones shown here will create a dramatically different result.

1 18-in (450mm) black chain

2 3 x ⅛-in (4mm) black jump rings

3 1 x ⅝-in (16mm) large antique black bolt ring

4 50 x 2-in (50mm) black head pins

5 50 x assorted shaped beads, 4–8mm in size

6 4 x 10-mm honeybee charms

Side or top cutters

Round-nose pliers

Snipe-nose pliers

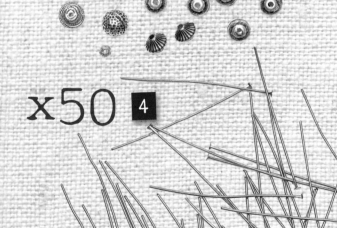

x50

honeybee

Assembling honeybee

1 Cut 2in (5cm) off the black chain. Cut the remaining 16in (40cm) in half, so that you have two 8-in (20cm) lengths. Add 1 x ⅛-in (4mm) jump ring to one end of one 8-in (20cm) length of chain, link on the large antique black bolt ring and then close. Add 1 x ⅛-in (4mm) jump ring to one end of the other 8-in (20cm) length of black chain, link on the other side of the antique black bolt ring and close.

2 Add 1 x ⅛-in (4mm) jump ring to the 2-in (5cm) length of chain, then link this to the other ends of both 8-in (20cm) lengths of chain and close, so that you have a necklace with a 2-in (5cm) dangle of chain at the centre front.

3 Now thread a head pin through a honeybee charm and, using round-nose pliers, make a hook as close to the top of the bee as possible.

4 Thread this hook through the very last link on the 2-in (5cm) dangle of chain and, holding the top of the hook with snipe-nose pliers, spiral the rest of the head pin around itself, securing the charm on the chain. Cut off any excess head pin.

5 Thread head pins through the largest beads, again making hooks as close to the tops of the beads as possible. If the hole of the bead is too large for your head pin, thread on a smaller bead first.

6 Thread the hooks at the tops of the beads made in step 5 randomly onto the chain and, as before, spiral the rest of the head pin around itself, securing all the beads onto the chain. Cut off any excess head pin.

7 Now repeat steps 5 and 6 with the remaining beads. There is no specific pattern, but it's nice to cluster the larger beads nearest the join of all the chains and use smaller beads as you work up the chain towards the clasp. As these beads are smaller, they will probably not require an extra bead to hold the eye pin.

8 Finally, following step 3, add the final three honeybee charms randomly to the chain so that they look as if they have just landed and are working busily away!

THINK ABOUT USING BEADS ALL EITHER MADE FROM THE SAME MATERIAL OR FROM THE SAME COLOUR PALETTE.

honeybee

la mer

Every day can feel like a summer's day
when you're wearing this sun-, sea- and
sand-inspired, striking necklace.

Everything you will need...

Attaching beads at intervals to a length of chain is a great way of obtaining a long necklace with a minimal amount of beads!

1. 9 x 2-in (50mm) silver eye pins
2. 9 x 30-mm large oval beads
3. 1 x 2-in (50mm) silver head pin
4. 1 x 7-mm nugget-shaped pearl
5. 16-in (400mm) silver trace chain
6. 1 x 20-mm starfish charm
7. 1 x 15-mm shell charm
8. 2 x 1/8-in (4mm) silver jump rings
9. 1 x 1/4-in (7mm) silver jump ring
10. 1 x 1/2-in (12mm) lobster clasp

Side or top cutters

Round-nose pliers

Snipe-nose pliers

la mer

Assembling la mer

1 Thread a silver eye pin through a large pearl oval bead and make a large eye loop as close to the top of the bead as possible.

2 Now thread the silver head pin through the nugget-shaped pearl and make a hook as close to the top of the pearl as possible. Link this hook onto the smaller loop of the eye pin on the oval bead.

3 Holding the hook with snipe-nose pliers, spiral the rest of the head pin around itself on top of the pearl, securing it firmly in place.

4 Thread an eye pin through another large bead and again make an eye loop as close to the top of the bead as possible. Try to keep the eye loop sizes the same and do not close them just yet. Repeat for the remaining seven beads.

5 Cut 8 x 1¼-in (3cm) lengths of chain from the silver trace chain, so that you are left with a 6-in (16cm) length. Cut this final piece in half, so that you also have 2 x 3-in (8cm) lengths of chain. Starting at the large pearl oval bead completed in step 3, thread a 1¼-in (3cm) length of chain onto the large eye loop made and then connect this piece of chain to the eye loop made on the next bead along, closing the loops as you go. Repeat this process until you have linked four beads on one side of the large pearl oval bead.

6 Starting again from the large pearl oval bead attach another 1¼-in (3cm) length of chain to the large eye loop and then connect this piece of chain to the next bead along and keep repeating for the remaining four beads to make the other side of the necklace. Add one 3-in (8cm) length of chain to the last bead on each side.

7 Re-open the large eye loop at the top of the large pearl oval bead now hanging at the centre front of your necklace and link on the starfish charm and close the loop. You can also link on a shell charm to an eye loop higher up the necklace for that extra maritime feel!

8 Finally, add 1 x ⅛-in (4mm) jump ring to each end of the 3-in (8cm) lengths of chain. Add a silver lobster clasp to one of the ⅛-in (4mm) jump rings and the ¼-in (7mm) silver jump ring to the other one before closing.

USING GORGEOUS DETAILED BEADS CAN REALLY GIVE A STRONG THEME TO A NECKLACE. AS EACH BEAD HAS ITS OWN SPACE AROUND IT.

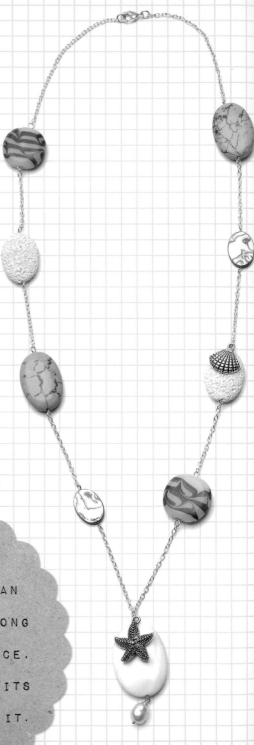

la mer

rainbow

Glass beads come in such an
array of beautiful colours that
I decided to make a feature of
them and create my own rainbow.

Everything you will need...

A wire choker is great for wiring beads on, as it is so rigid.

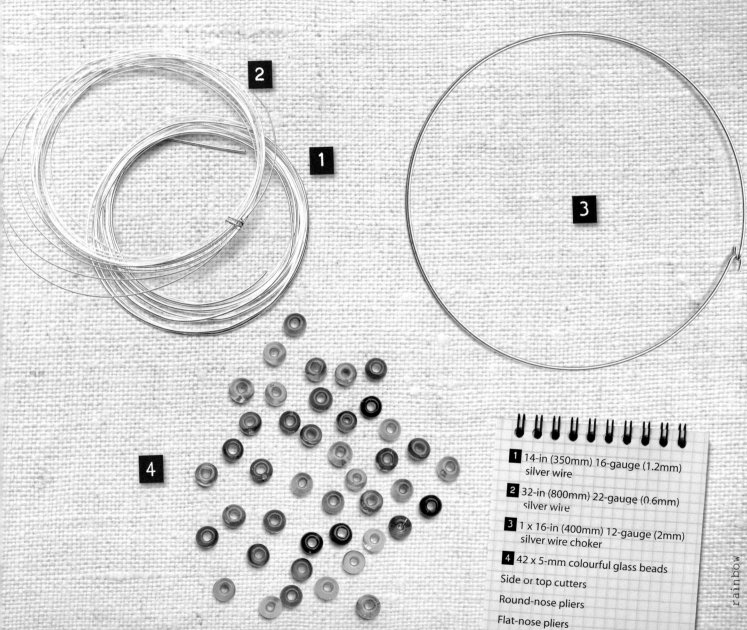

1 14-in (350mm) 16-gauge (1.2mm) silver wire

2 32-in (800mm) 22-gauge (0.6mm) silver wire

3 1 x 16-in (400mm) 12-gauge (2mm) silver wire choker

4 42 x 5-mm colourful glass beads

Side or top cutters

Round-nose pliers

Flat-nose pliers

rainbow

Assembling rainbow

1 Cut a 14-in (35cm) length of 16-gauge (1.2mm) silver wire and start to form a loop at one end, using the very base of your round-nose pliers.

2 Manipulating the wire around this loop, gently bend the wire to form a loose spiral. This is probably easier to do with your fingers rather than using pliers. Continue to spiral the wire so that it goes around the central loop at least twice. When you are happy with the shape, bend the wire away from the spiral at an angle of 90 degrees using your flat-nose pliers. This should leave you with a length of at least 2in (5cm) of wire in preparation for step 3.

3 Using your round-nose pliers, form an eye loop ¹/₂in (1cm) up from the 90-degree bend you made in step 2. Do not cut away the excess wire yet.

4 Cut a 12-in (30cm) length of 22-gauge (0.6mm) wire and lay one end against the thicker wire, just below the eye loop that you made in step 3. Start to wrap the remaining 16-gauge (1.2mm wire) around the thinner wire and itself, so that you are trapping the thin wire underneath. When you reach the start of the curve of your spiral, cut away the excess 16-gauge (1.2mm) wire and the excess 22-gauge (0.6mm) wire that is sticking out at the top of the eye loop.

5 Wrap the thinner wire around the thicker one a couple of times to get it in position at the top of the spiral. Add your first glass bead and then wrap the thin wire twice around the thick wire.

6 Add another bead and again wrap the thin wire twice around the thicker wire. Continue to add more beads in this way until you come to the loop that you made in step 1 at the centre of the spiral. Wrap the thin wire around the thicker wire a couple of times and cut off any excess.

7 Thread the spiral pendant onto the 12-gauge (2mm) wire choker from the eye loop you completed in step 4 and centre it at the bottom. Cut an 8-in (20cm) length of 22-gauge (0.6mm) wire and wrap it around the wire choker several times immediately to the right of the pendant.

8 Add a glass bead and wrap the thin wire twice around the choker to the right-hand side of the pendant. Repeat this process until you have added ten glass beads. When you have added the last bead, wrap the remaining thin wire several times around the wire choker to secure itself and cut off any excess.

9 Repeat steps 7–9 to add ten beads to the left-hand side of the pendant.

SPIRAL A LENGTH OF THICK WIRE TO CREATE A PENDANT AS A FOCAL POINT FOR YOUR NECKLACE. YOU CAN WIRE BEADS ONTO THAT, TOO!

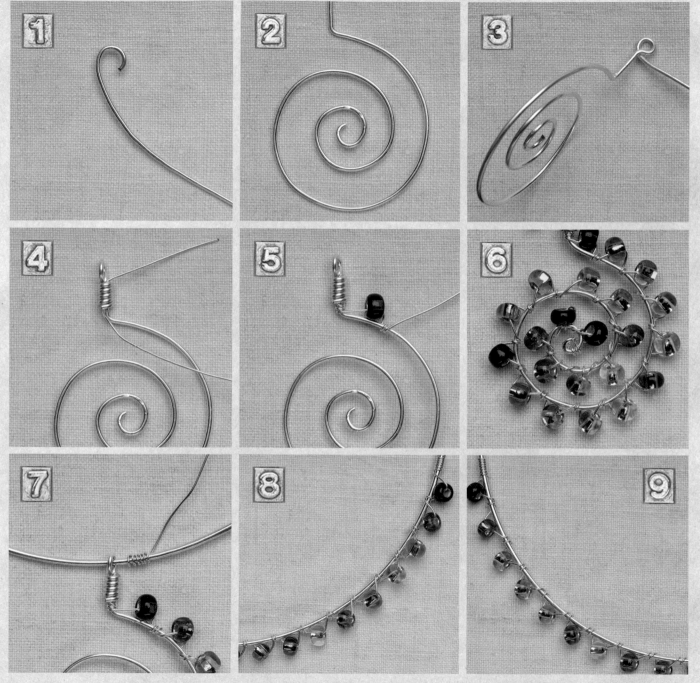

military

Chain and beads in these muted colours have a military look and made me think of medals, giving me the idea of having all the chains hanging down.

Everything you will need...

Combining lots of different styles of chain can create a big impact. Using a wire choker as your starting point will keep all the chains hanging beautifully, as it can take all the weight.

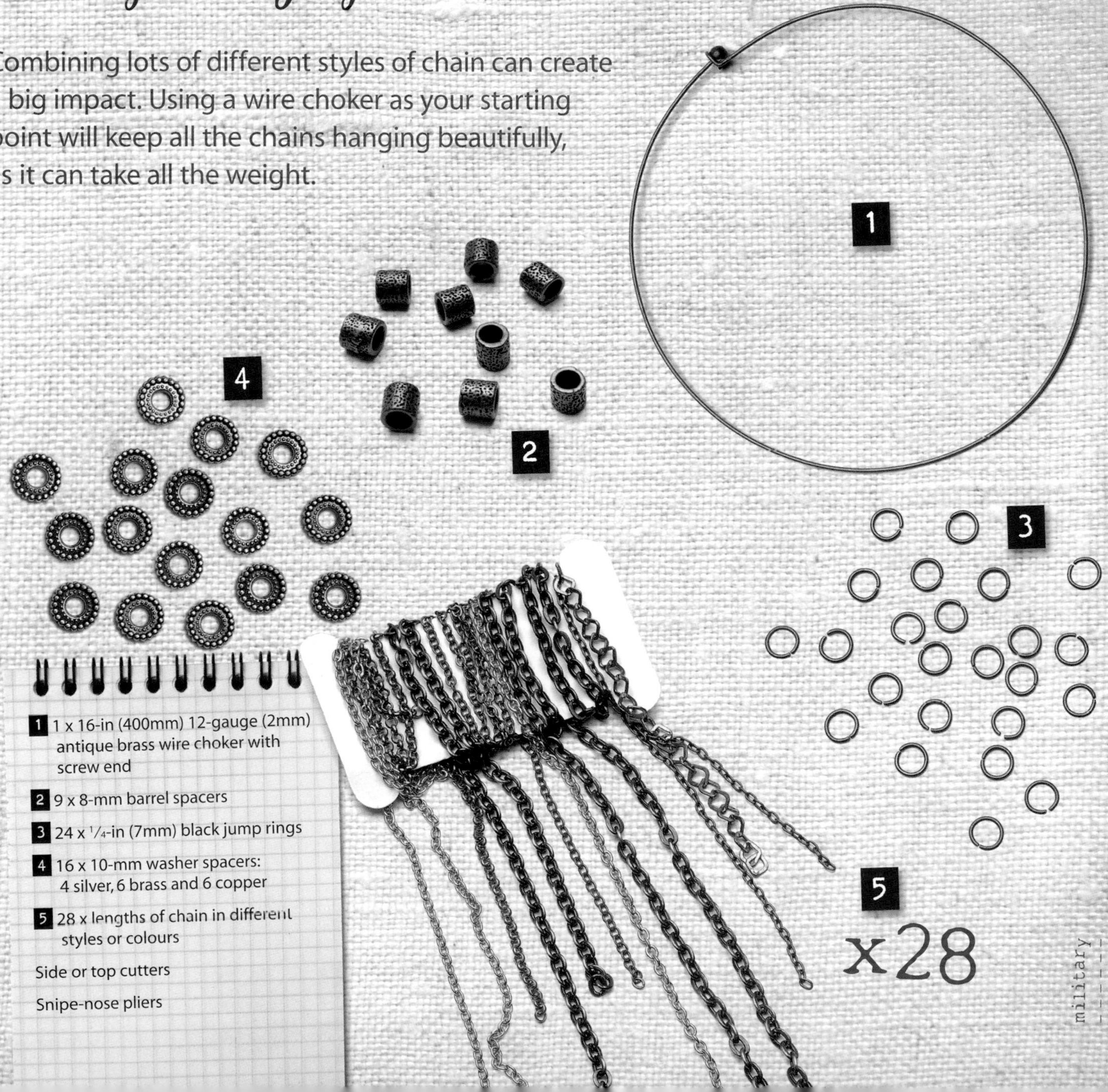

1 1 x 16-in (400mm) 12-gauge (2mm) antique brass wire choker with screw end

2 9 x 8-mm barrel spacers

3 24 x ¼-in (7mm) black jump rings

4 16 x 10-mm washer spacers: 4 silver, 6 brass and 6 copper

5 28 x lengths of chain in different styles or colours

Side or top cutters

Snipe-nose pliers

x28

military

Assembling military

1 Unscrew the ball at the end of the wire choker and place it somewhere safe.

2 Now add onto the wire choker the following sequence: 1 x barrel spacer, 1 x jump ring, 1 x washer spacer, 1 x jump ring, 1 x washer spacer, 1 x jump ring. Repeat this sequence seven more times and then add on the last barrel spacer. Screw the ball end of the choker back on in order to secure everything in place.

3 Start by adding the chain loop detail to the jump rings. It's best to use your darkest, heaviest chain for this, as the loops will stand out. You can make the chain as long as you like. I started with a 4-in (10cm) drop, opened the jump ring between the first two washer spacers on the left-hand side, linked on the chain and then closed the jump ring.

4 Then loop the chain, linking it to the jump ring between the fifth set of washer spacers from the left-hand side. (You can make this loop any size you like.) Cut off any excess chain.

5 Repeat steps 3 and 4, this time working from the right-hand side to create a symmetrical pattern of two loops crossing each other at the middle of the choker.

6 Take another length of dark chain and link it to the jump ring between the second set of washer spacers from the left-hand side, remembering to leave approximately 4in (10cm) hanging down. Then loop it to the jump ring in the middle of the sixth set of washer spacers from the left. Cut off any excess chain and repeat from the right-hand side to complete all the hanging loops.

7 Now add different colours and patterns of chain to the remaining jump rings. If the chain is quite fine, you can add two lengths of chain onto the same jump ring.

8 Finally, shape the bottom of the chain lengths. The easiest way to do this is to hang the choker on a door handle, for example, and tape a piece of paper behind it that has a diagonal line drawn on it, then use side or top cutters to cut all the chains to follow the drawn line.

THIS IS A GREAT WAY TO USE BROKEN BITS OF CHAIN. THE MORE STYLES AND COLOURS OF CHAIN YOU USE, THE MORE INTERESTING THE DESIGN.

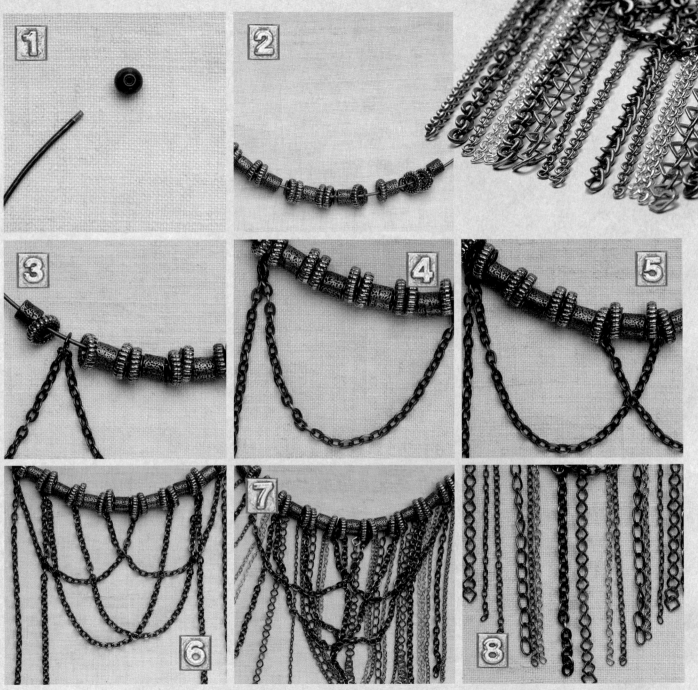

fabric,
ribbons
and thong

knotty

This necklace is great as there is
no need for any findings at all
— the beads are all that matter!

Everything you will need...

I have played on the knotting theme and chosen beads that are all made from knots and cord. Try to keep the distance between each bead the same.

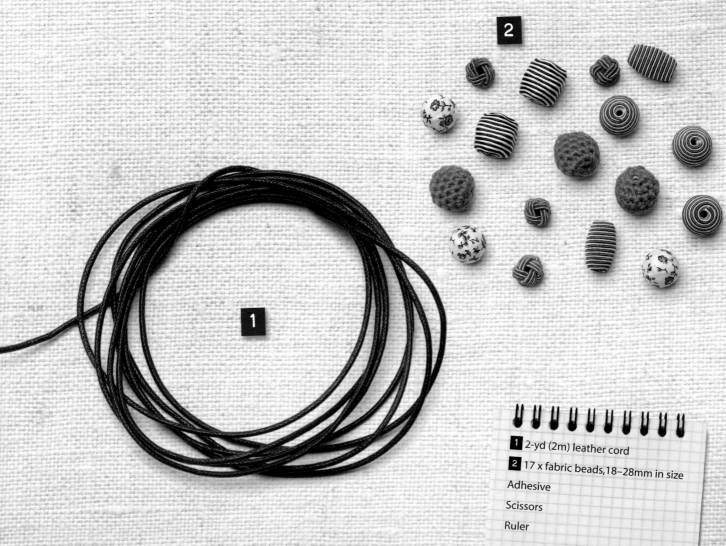

1. 2-yd (2m) leather cord
2. 17 x fabric beads, 18–28mm in size
   Adhesive
   Scissors
   Ruler

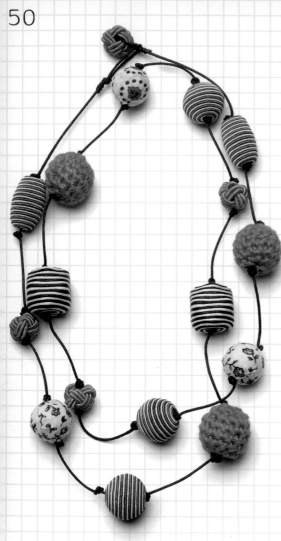

Assembling knotty

1 At one end of the leather cord, make a loop large enough for one of your beads to pass through. When you have made the loop the right size, tie a knot in the cord to secure the loop size and set the bead to one side. Cut away the excess cord $^1/_2$in (1cm) from the knot. Apply a drop of adhesive to the knot and wrap the short end of the cord around the long length to finish the knot off neatly.

2 Lay your cord against a ruler and tie a knot approximately $2^3/_4$in (7cm) along from your knotted loop.

3 Slide the first bead along the leather cord until it rests on the knot you have just made. Tie another knot directly after the bead to hold it in place on the cord.

4 Tie another knot $1^1/_4$in (3cm) along the leather cord from the bead. Add another bead, slide it along to meet this knot and tie another knot directly after it.

5 Continue tying knots and adding beads until there is only the one bead left that fitted the loop you made in step 1. Add this final bead and place it on the leather cord $2^3/_4$in (7cm) along from the last bead.

6 Take the end of the leather cord and tie a knot under the final bead to secure it in place. As in step 1, cut away the excess cord $^1/_2$in (1cm) from the knot. Apply a drop of adhesive to the knot and wrap the short end of the cord around the long length to finish the knot off neatly.

LAY OUT ALL YOUR BEADS FIRST TO CALCULATE HOW LONG YOU WANT TO MAKE YOUR NECKLACE AND DETERMINE THE LENGTH OF LEATHER CORD BETWEEN EACH BEAD.

ADDING A DROP OF ADHESIVE TO THE END OF YOUR
LEATHER CORD SETS IT HARD, SO THAT IT IS
EASY TO THREAD THROUGH THE BEADS.

knotty

These pretty bird beads in rows remind me of birds singing on the telephone wires in the morning.

songbird

Everything you will need...

Using strips of fabric to create a necklace
is a funky alternative to wearing a scarf.

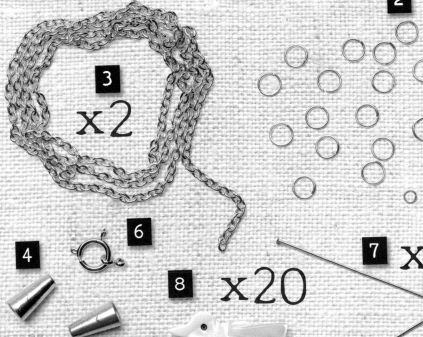

2

3 x2

5

4

6

8 x20

7 x20

x4 **1**

9 x20

10

Scissors

Flat-nose pliers

Needle and thread

Two–part adhesive

Round-nose pliers

Side or top cutters

1 4 x 32-in (800mm) strips of fabric ³⁄₄in (20mm) wide

2 20 x ¹⁄₄-in (7mm) jump rings

3 2 x 2-in (50mm) lengths of silver trace chain

4 2 x 15-mm silver cone chain ends

5 2 x ¹⁄₈-in (4mm) silver jump rings

6 1 x ¹⁄₂-in (12mm) large silver bolt ring

7 20 x 2-in (50mm) silver head pins

8 20 x 18-mm bird-shaped beads

9 20 x 2-in (50mm) silver eye pins

10 20 x 4-mm bicone crystal beads

songbird

Assembling songbird

1 Cut four strips of fabric 32in (80cm) long and ³/₄in (20mm) wide. I used an old jersey T-shirt. Measure in and mark 6in (16cm) from either end of each strip and then loosely tie five knots between these two measurements. It doesn't matter if the knots are not evenly spaced.

2 When you are happy with the position of your knots, link a ¼-in (7mm) jump ring into each one, close it and pull the knot tightly.

3 Gather your four lengths together and arrange them as shown, so that the fabric lengths are staggered. When you are happy with their positioning, cut away the excess fabric so that all the ends are even.

4 Pinch together all the ends of the fabric as tightly as possible and sew them to each other. Check that they fit inside the cone end, then sew on one length of trace chain at the very end of the gathered fabrics. Repeat for the other side of the necklace.

5 Next, following the manufacturer's instructions, mix the two-part adhesive and apply it to the fabric ends that you have sewn. Thread the chain through the cone chain end and pull it, so that the fabric ends are pulled into the cone and all the stitching is hidden. Repeat for the other side of the necklace.

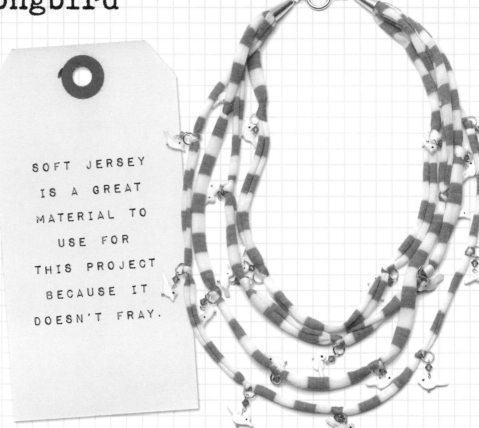

SOFT JERSEY IS A GREAT MATERIAL TO USE FOR THIS PROJECT BECAUSE IT DOESN'T FRAY.

6 Make sure that you have one link of chain sticking out of each cone chain end and cut away all the rest. Add 1 x ¹/₈-in (4mm) jump ring to each link of exposed chain. Add a bolt ring between the two jump rings.

7 Thread a head pin through a bird bead and make an eye loop as close to the top of the bird as possible. Repeat for all the remaining beads.

8 Thread an eye pin through a 4-mm bicone crystal and make an eye loop as close to the top of the bead as possible. Repeat for all the remaining beads.

9 Join the bird bead and crystal together by the eye loops and close. Then re-open one of the ¼-in (7mm) jump rings, link through the top eye loop on the crystal bead and close. Repeat this step to add all the bird beads.

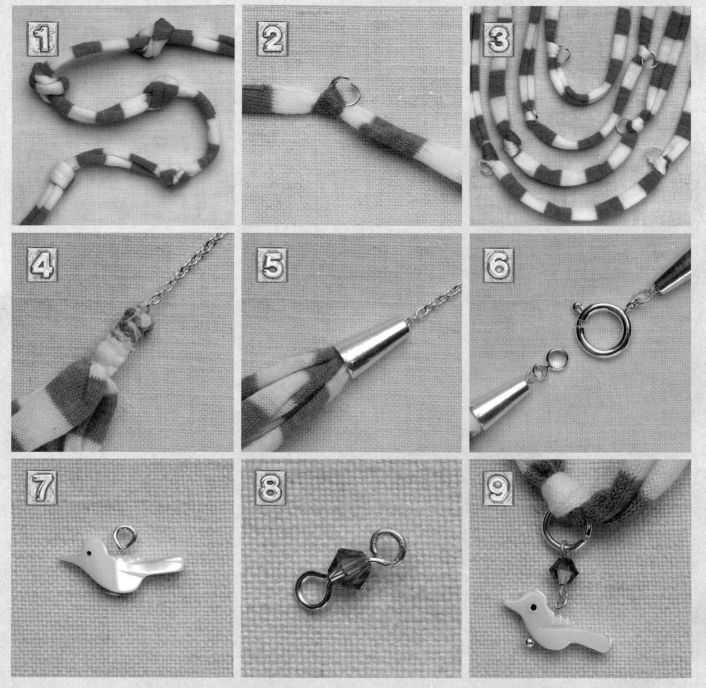

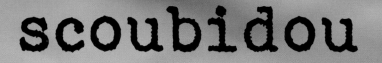

scoubidou

The way you plait and knot
leather and suede cords can
create many different patterns.

Everything you will need...

In this design I have adapted a fad from my youth called scoubidou, which originally used thin plastic tubes. I have applied the technique to lengths of suede to give it a modern twist.

1. 6-yd (6m) blue suede ribbon, $^1/_8$in (3mm) wide

2. 6-yd (6m) pink suede ribbon, $^1/_8$in (3mm) wide

3. 4 x 12-mm crystal charm spacer beads

4. 3 x 12-mm flower charm spacer beads

5. 1 x $^3/_4$-in (20mm) clasp

Scissors

Masking tape

Two-part adhesive

scoubidou

Assembling scoubidou

1 Cut your lengths of ribbon in half, so you have 2 x 3-yd (3m) lengths of each colour. Holding the four lengths at one end, wrap a little piece of masking tape around the ends to hold them all together. Then holding the masking taped ends, fan the suede lengths out to form a cross shape, ensuring the colours alternate.

2 Working in a clockwise direction, loop the top pink length of suede over the length of blue suede to its right.

3 Take this blue length of suede and loop it over the bottom pink length.

4 Then take this pink length and loop it over the blue length of suede to its left.

5 Finally take this last blue length and thread it through the loop you made with the first pink length of suede in step 2.

6 Pull all four lengths of suede and they will come together tightly to form a small neat square of alternating colours.

7 Repeat steps 2–6 over and over, so that you start to form a tight spiral of suede. When you have built up a length of 2in (5cm), thread all four lengths of suede through the hole of the first crystal charm spacer bead. Slide the bead along the suede until it meets the spiral.

8 Repeat steps 2–6 to create another 2in (5cm) of spiralled suede, then thread all four lengths of suede through the hole on a flower-shaped spacer bead.

9 Repeat steps 7 and 8, alternating crystal charm and flower spacer beads, until you have a 16-in (40cm) spiral of suede with the spacer beads every 2in (5cm). Trim all the suede ends so that they are the same length, wrapping a piece of masking tape around them to temporarily hold them in place. Mix up some two-part adhesive and place it in the ends of the large clasp. Remove the masking tape from each end of the suede and push the suede ends into the clasp and hold until set.

USE BEADS WITH REALLY LARGE HOLES, SO THAT YOU CAN THREAD THEM EASILY OVER THE LEATHER AND SUEDE CORDS.

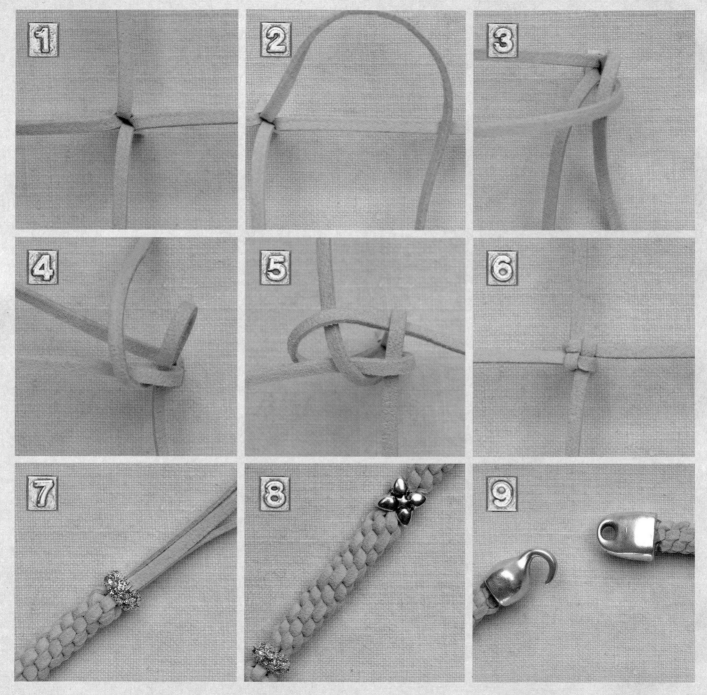

cameo

Take inspiration from the Victorian era and use velvet ribbon to hold a 'cameo' – one of the Victorians' favourite pieces of jewellery.

Everything you will need...

Diamante buckles come in a variety of shapes, so you can make your necklace truly unique.

1 1 x ½-in (12mm) round diamante buckle

2 14-in (350mm) black velvet ribbon, ⅝in (15mm) wide

3 2 x ½-in (12mm) large ribbon crimps

4 2 x ⅛-in (4mm) oval jump rings

5 1 x ¼-in (7mm) jump ring

6 1 x ½ in (12mm) lobster clasp

7 1 x 2-in (50mm) chain extender

8 2 x 2-in (50mm) eye pins

9 1 x 20-mm cameo bead

10 1 x 10-mm black rose bead

11 1 x 4-mm diamante round charm

Flat-nose pliers

Round-nose pliers

Top or side cutters

Scissors

cameo

Assembling cameo

1 Thread the diamante buckle onto the length of velvet ribbon.

2 Place one end of the velvet ribbon in the jaws of a ribbon crimp. If the ribbon crimp is smaller than the width of your ribbon, just gather the ribbon slightly so that it fits in nicely. There are teeth on the jaws of ribbon crimps, so it's quite easy to hold the ribbon in place. Squash the jaws of the crimp tightly together using flat-nose pliers.

3 Place the ribbon around your neck and mark where you need to place the other ribbon crimp. You may need to cut away excess ribbon at this point. Repeat step 2 to attach the other ribbon crimp to the other end of the velvet. Attach a $1/8$-in (4mm) oval jump ring and lobster clasp to one end. Attach the other $1/8$-in (4mm) oval jump ring and a $1/4$-in (7mm) jump ring holding the chain extender to the other end.

4 Thread an eye pin through your cameo bead and make a large eye loop as close to the top of the cameo as possible. Thread this eye loop through the back of the diamante buckle and close. Centre the diamante buckle on the black velvet ribbon so that the cameo dangles at the front.

5 Thread an eye pin through the rose bead and make an eye loop as close to the top as possible. Link it to the bottom eye loop on the cameo and close. Link the diamante charm to the bottom eye loop on the rose and close.

USING A CHAIN EXTENDER IS A GREAT IDEA WITH THIS STYLE OF NECKLACE. IT ENABLES YOU TO ADJUST THE LENGTH OF THE CHOKER EASILY TO FIT ANY SIZE OF NECK.

linking
beads

stella

Stella is the Latin word for 'star'.
It sprang to mind when I saw these
stripy blue beads, as they reminded
me of mini planets - so I looked to
the night sky for inspiration.

Everything you will need...

Bead cups are available in many colours and shapes and can add that extra finishing touch to a design.

3

1

x18

9

2

8

7

6

10

5

4

1 18 x 2-in (50mm) silver eye pins
2 22 x 12-mm bead cups
3 11 x 18-mm blue agate beads
4 7-in (180mm) silver chain
5 11 x 5/8-in (16mm) closed twisted jump rings
6 2 x 3/8-in (10mm) twisted jump rings
7 2 x 1/4-in (6mm) twisted jump rings
8 1 x 3/4-in (20mm) star toggle clasp
9 7 x 13-mm star beads
10 7 x 10-mm star charms

Round-nose pliers

Top or side cutters

Flat-nose pliers

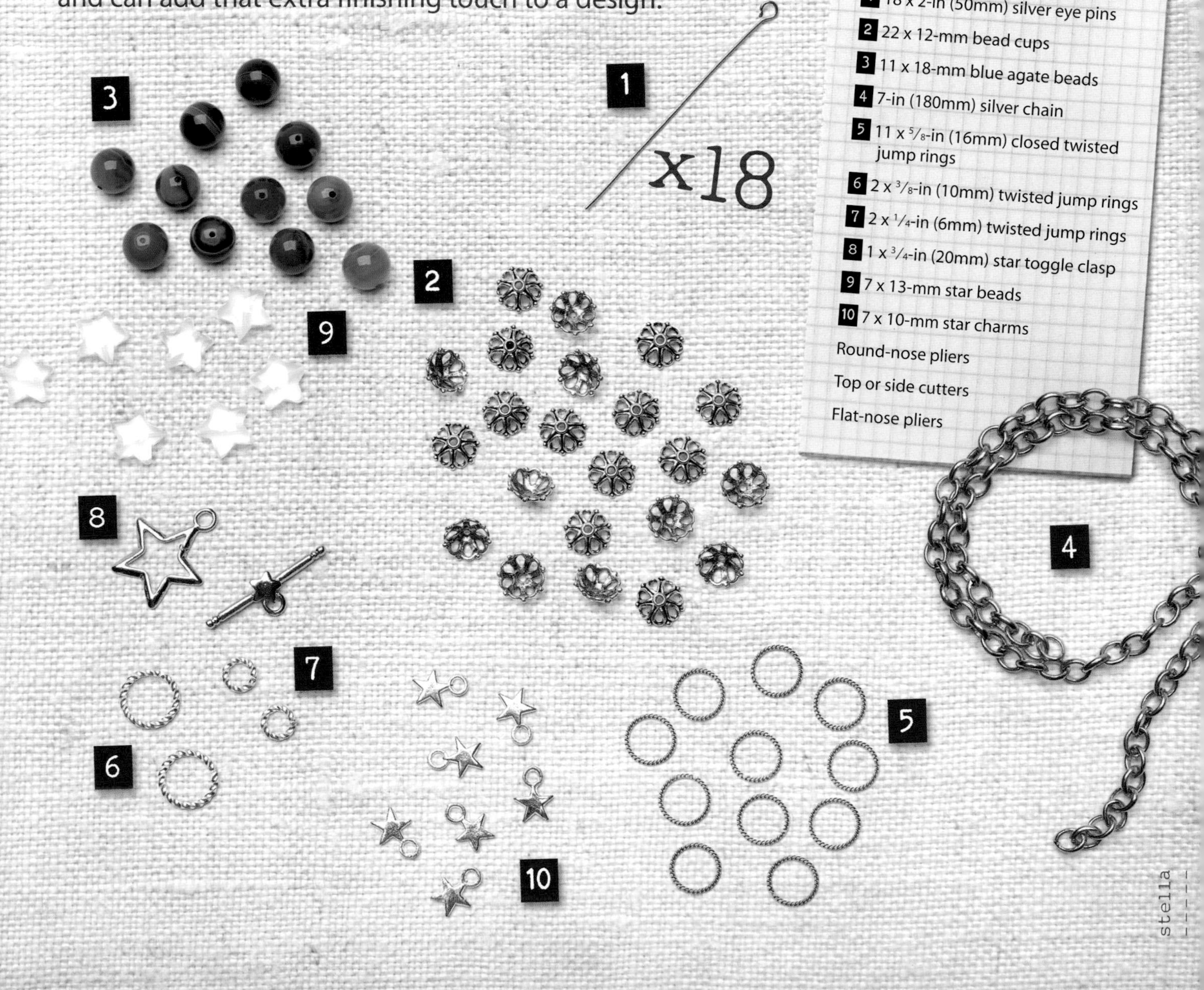

stella

Assembling stella

1 Thread an eye pin through a bead cup, then thread on a blue agate bead followed by another bead cup.

2 Form an eye loop as close to the top of the second bead cup as possible and cut away any excess wire. Do not fully close this eye loop just yet. Repeat steps 1 and 2 for the other ten agate beads.

3 Cut the silver chain into three 2³/₈-in (6cm) lengths. Thread the last link of each piece onto one of the open eye loops you made on one of the agate beads in step 2 and close.

4 Keeping hold of this same bead, re-open the eye loop at the other end of this bead, thread on 1 x ⁵/₈-in (16mm) twisted jump ring and reclose the eye loop.

5 Take another of the agate beads completed in step 2, thread it onto the same ⁵/₈-in (16mm) jump ring and close the eye loop. Repeat this step so that you have two agate beads joined to the same twisted jump ring.

6 Open the eye loops at the other end of the beads you have just added, thread another ⁵/₈-in (16mm) twisted jump ring onto each one and close. Repeat this pattern of agate bead and ⁵/₈-in (16mm) jump ring until you have five agate beads on each side of the central pendant bead holding the three lengths of chain.

7 Open a ³/₈-in (10mm) twisted jump ring, link it onto the last ⁵/₈-in (16mm) jump ring on each side of the necklace, then add a ¹/₄-in (6mm) twisted jump ring on each side and close. Then open the ¹/₄-in (6mm) twisted jump ring on one side of the necklace and link on one part of a star toggle clasp. Repeat this step on the other side to attach the other part of the toggle clasp.

8 Attach a star charm to the loop of an eye pin and close, then thread this eye pin through a star bead and form a hook as close to the top of the star bead as possible. Thread this hook through one of the links on one of the lengths of chain attached to the bottom bead. Bend the length of wire around to form a closed eye loop, securing the star bead and charm in place. Cut off any excess wire.

9 Repeat step 8, attaching star beads and charms to all three lengths of chain in a random pattern. Cut off any excess chain at the bottom of each length once you've added all the beads, so that the chains are different lengths.

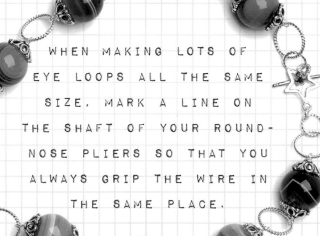

WHEN MAKING LOTS OF EYE LOOPS ALL THE SAME SIZE, MARK A LINE ON THE SHAFT OF YOUR ROUND-NOSE PLIERS SO THAT YOU ALWAYS GRIP THE WIRE IN THE SAME PLACE.

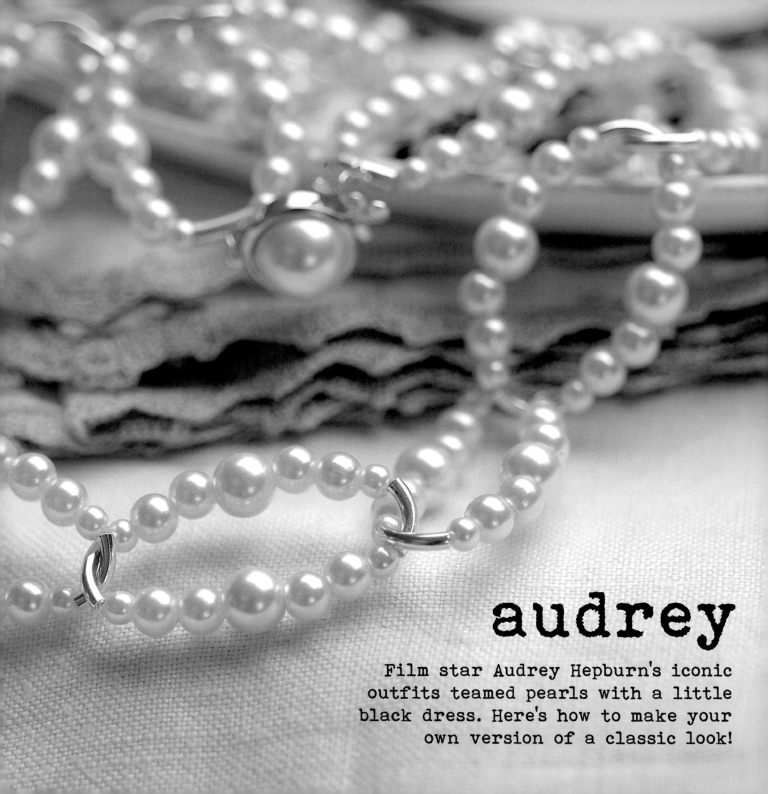

audrey

Film star Audrey Hepburn's iconic
outfits teamed pearls with a little
black dress. Here's how to make your
own version of a classic look!

Everything you will need...

Joining beads to make actual links gives
an unusual twist to simple stringing.

5

7

1

x28

2

1 26 x 10-mm curved noodle
spacer tubes

2 28 x 8-mm pearls

3 112 x 6-mm pearls

4 56 x 4-mm pearls

5 2 x 10-mm curved noodle bails

6 1 x roll of $1/64$-in (0.3mm)
nylon thread

7 1 x $5/8$-in (15mm) pearl clasp

Scissors

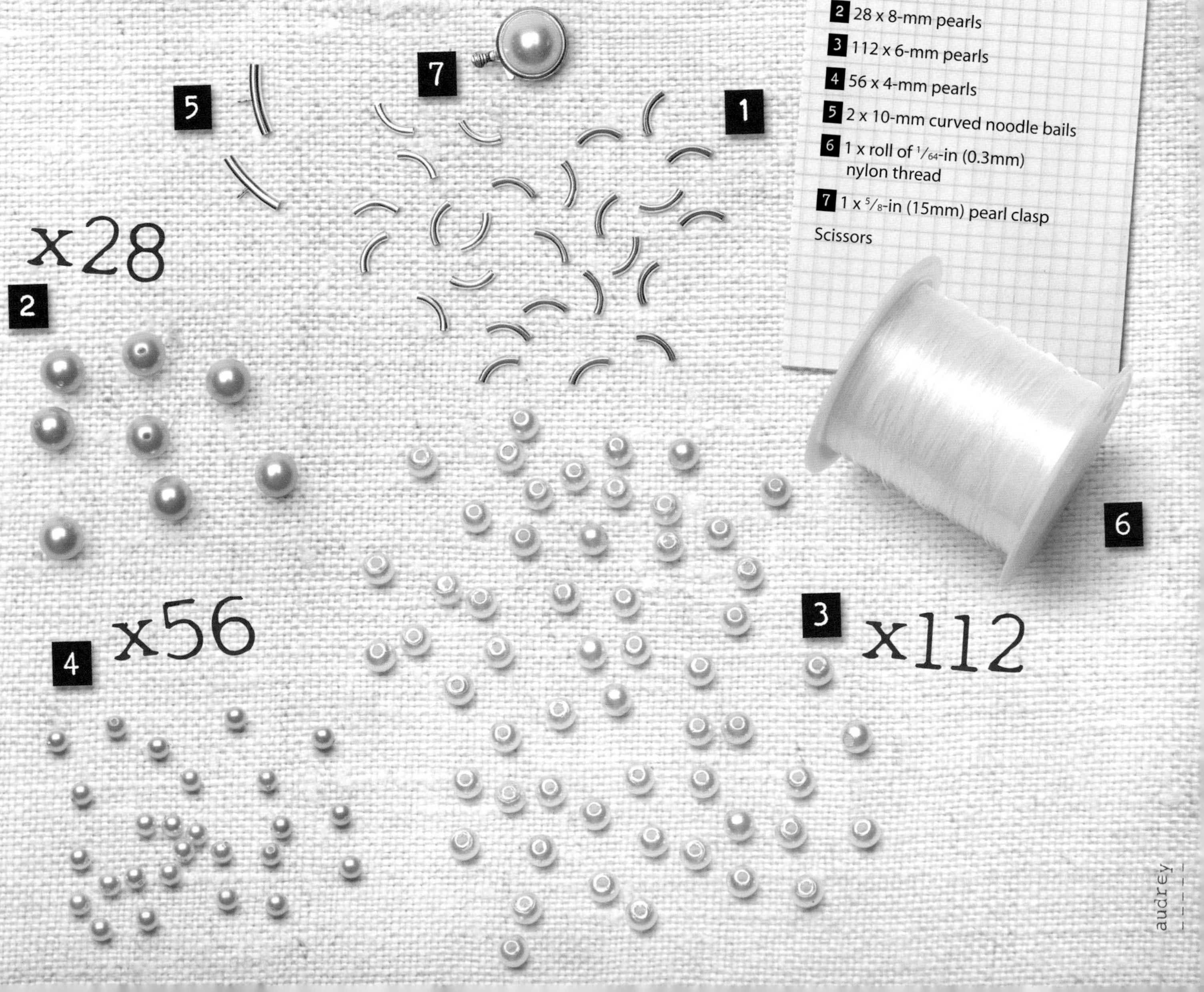

6

3 x112

4 x56

audrey

Assembling audrey

1 Place 2 x curved noodle spacer tubes, 2 x 8-mm pearls, 8 x 6-mm pearls and 4 x 4-mm pearls on a bead mat, laid out as shown in the photo.

2 Cut a 12-in (30cm) length of nylon thread from the roll and thread on all the beads in the order shown in step 1.

3 When all the beads are on, thread one end of the nylon back through all the beads so that it comes round to meet the other end again.

4 Tie a double knot, pulling all the beads together tightly. The noodle spacers at either end will give the overall piece an oval shape. Then thread the ends of the nylon thread back through a couple of the beads and cut off any excess. This prevents you from cutting the nylon too close to the original knot.

5 Cut another 12-in (30cm) length of nylon and thread on the same formation of beads as in step 1. Then pass one end of the nylon through the first 'beaded link' that you completed in step 4.

6 Pass one end of the nylon back through all the beads to meet the other end; you have now joined two 'links' together. Repeat step 4 to tie the knot and secure. Repeat steps 5 and 6 until you have made 12 joined beaded links.

7 You now need to make the final two links to add to either end of the necklace. Repeat steps 5 and 6, replacing one noodle spacer tube in each 'link' with a noodle bail.

8 Attach a pearl clasp to the noodle bail at each end of the necklace and close.

LOOK OUT FOR VINTAGE CLASPS ON PIECES OF OLD JEWELLERY FROM CHARITY SHOPS TO GIVE YOUR NECKLACE A UNIQUE FEEL.

audrey
- - - - -

harvest

Acorn charms inspired this
autumnal-looking necklace
in rich browns and golds.

Everything you will need...

Changing the charms and colour scheme for this style of necklace can create endless design possibilities.

1. 2 x 40-in (1m) 1/64-in (0.3mm) clear nylon thread
2. 1 x 1 3/8-in (35mm) ring
3. 46 x gold 3-mm beads
4. 10 x 5/8-in (15mm) filigree bead cups
5. 1 x 15-mm black bead
6. 48 x 7-mm black bugle beads
7. 288 x brown seed beads
8. 48 x matt gold seed beads
9. 6 x large feature beads, 25–40mm in size: 2 gold, 2 green, 2 smoke
10. 6 x 8-mm black beads
11. 2 x crimp tubes
12. 1 x 1-in (25mm) toggle clasp
13. 2 x 1/8-in (3mm) crimp covers
14. 8-in (200mm) gold curb chain
15. 3 x 30-mm acorn charms
16. 4 x 18-mm leaf charms
17. 1 x 25-mm gold daisy charm
18. 2 x 2-in (50mm) gold head pins
19. 5 x 1/8-in (5mm) gold jump rings

Scissors

Crimping pliers

Snipe-nose pliers

Side or top cutters

Round-nose pliers

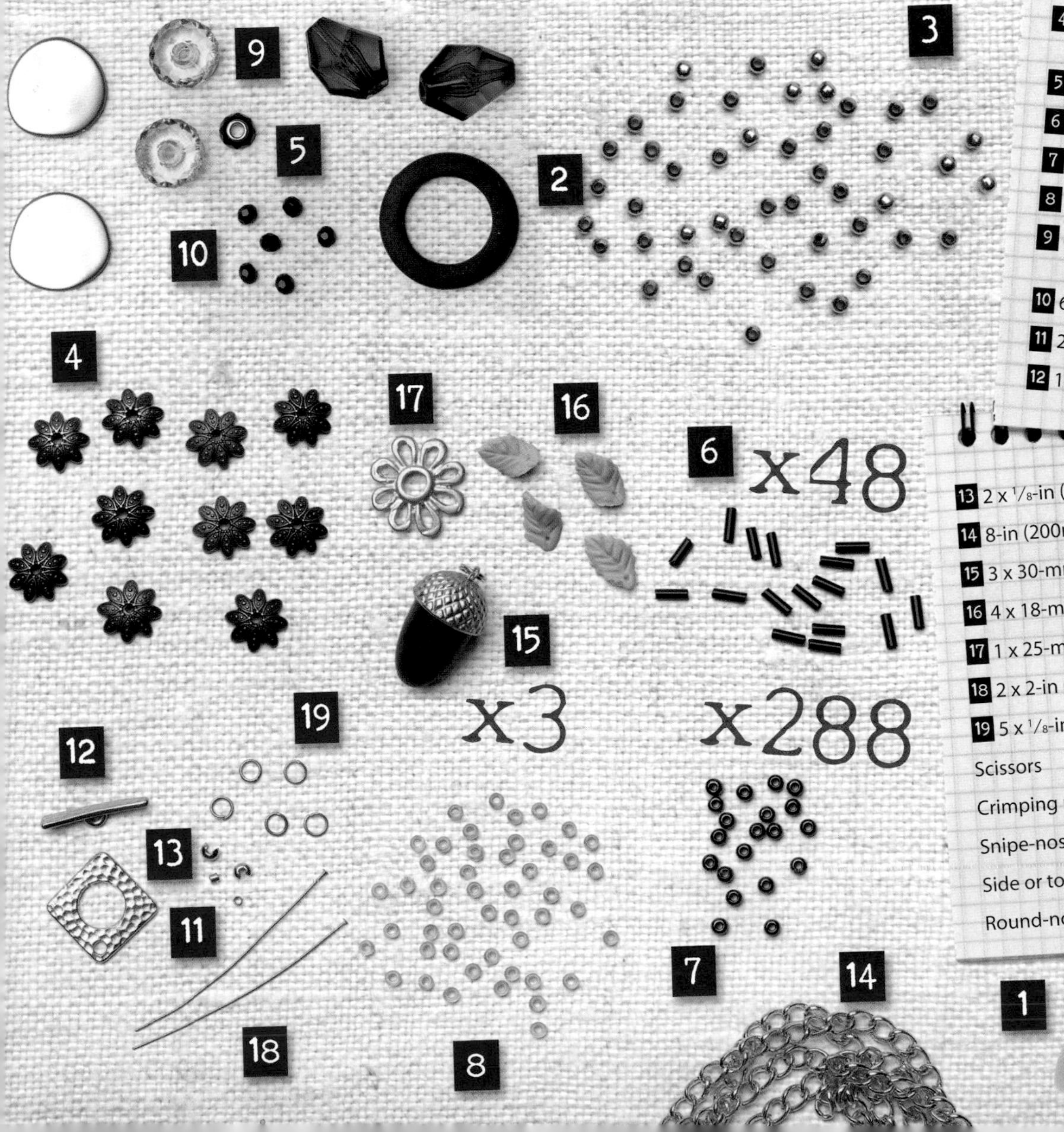

x48

x3

x288

harvest

Assembling harvest

1 Holding both 40-in (1m) lengths of nylon, fold them in half so that each piece is 20in (50cm) long. Place the looped ends of the nylon across the 1³/₈-in (35mm) ring, pass the other ends of nylon through the middle of the ring and then through the nylon loops, and pull to secure. Check that you have four lengths of nylon coming off the ring.

2 Thread all four ends through 1 x 3-mm gold bead and slide the bead down the nylon to meet the ring. Then add 1 x bead cup, 1 x 15-mm black bead, 1 x bead cup and 1 x 3-mm gold bead, again threading all four ends of nylon through the beads at the same time.

3 Now separate the nylon threads and start beading onto each length in turn. Add 1 x black bugle bead, 5 x brown seed beads, 1 x matt gold seed bead, 1 x brown seed bead, 1 x 3-mm gold bead, 1 x brown seed bead, 1 x matt gold seed bead, 5 x brown seed beads and 1 x black bugle bead onto each length.

4 Regroup two of the nylon threads and thread them both through 1 x 3-mm gold bead, 1 x bead cup, 1 x feature bead, 1 x bead cup and 1 x 3-mm gold bead. Repeat for the other two nylon threads.

5 Repeat steps 3 and 4 using all your feature beads and 4 x 8-mm black beads until the necklace is the length you require.

6 When you have the right length, thread on a crimp tube, then pass the nylon through the loop on the toggle clasp and back through the crimp tube.

7 Pull the nylon to ensure that all the beads meet the crimp tube and are snug along the nylon strands. Using crimping pliers, squash the crimp tube and slide a crimp cover over the tube to make it look like a 3-mm gold bead. Repeat steps 6 and 7 to add the other part of the toggle clasp to the other side of the necklace.

8 Fold the gold curb chain in half and attach it to the ring in the same way as you added the nylon in step 1, so that you have two lengths of chain dangling from the ring. Attach an acorn charm by threading its loop through two of the links on the curb chain to secure the chain in place. Add the other acorns, one on either side.

9 Using ¹/₈-in (5mm) jump rings, add the daisy charm and leaves near the top of the ring to create a cluster of objects. Finally, thread head pins through two of the 8-mm black beads, form a hook at the tops of the beads and thread them through the last link of each length of chain. Spiral the excess length of the head pins onto the tops of the beads to secure them in place. Cut away any excess headpin.

butterfly

These elegant connectors came in
so many shapes, sizes and colours
that they inspired me to use them
on their own to create a flutter
of butterflies around your neck!

Everything you will need...

Oval jump rings enable you to space beads further apart, without creating the width that a round jump ring would.

1 3 x $1^1/_2$-in (38mm) brass butterfly connectors

2 16 x $^3/_{16}$-in (4mm) oval antique brass jump rings

3 2 x $^7/_8$-in (22mm) light blue, 2 x dark blue and 2 x green butterfly connectors

4 1 x $1^5/_8$-in (42mm) black butterfly connector

5 $^1/_2$-in (12mm) length of antique brass small-link chain

6 2 x $^1/_4$-in (7mm) antique brass jump rings

7 1 x 2-in (50mm) antique brass head pin

8 1 x 4-mm green bicone crystal

9 1 x 2-in (50mm) antique brass eye pin

10 1 x 8-mm blue nugget pearl

11 2 x 4-in (100mm) lengths of antique brass large-link chain

12 1 x $^1/_2$-in (12mm) antique brass lobster clasp

Snipe-nose pliers

Flat-nose pliers

Side or top cutters

Round-nose pliers

x2

butterfly

Assembling butterfly

1 Link the three 1¹⁄₂-in (38mm) brass butterfly connectors together, using 1 x ¹⁄₈-in (4mm) oval antique brass jump ring at the tip of each wing.

2 Add another ¹⁄₈-in (4mm) oval jump ring to the tips of the outer butterflies' wings and link one small light blue butterfly connector to each end.

3 Add another ¹⁄₈-in (4mm) oval jump ring to the tips of the light blue butterflies' wings and link one small dark blue butterfly connector to each end.

4 Take a small green butterfly connector and add 1 x ¹⁄₈-in (4mm) oval jump ring to the tip of each wing. Link these two oval jump rings halfway between the centre and the right-hand brass butterflies. Repeat this step to attach the other small green butterfly connector between the centre and left-hand brass butterflies.

5 Take the large black butterfly connector and add 1 x ¹⁄₈-in (4mm) oval jump ring to the tip of each wings. Link these two jump rings in between the two small green butterflies, about halfway up their bottom wings.

6 Thread the ¹⁄₂-in (12mm) length of small-link chain onto 1 x ¹⁄₄-in (7mm) jump ring and link the jump ring to the hole at the centre of the large black butterfly.

7 Thread the head pin through the 4-mm green bicone crystal, make an eye loop as close to the top of the bead as possible and close. Thread an eye pin through the 8-mm blue nugget pearl and make an eye loop as close to the other side of the bead as possible. Attach the crystal to this eye loop and close. Open the eye loop on the other side of the blue nugget pearl, link it to the last link of the ¹⁄₂-in (12mm) chain and close.

8 Thread 1 x ¹⁄₈-in (4mm) oval jump ring onto the end of one of the 4-in (10cm) lengths of large-link chain and link it to the tip of a dark blue butterfly wing. Repeat for the other side of the necklace.

9 Add 1 x ¹⁄₈-in (4mm) oval jump ring and 1 x ¹⁄₄-in (7mm) jump ring to one end of the chain and 1 x ¹⁄₈-in (4rnm) oval jump ring and the lobster clasp to the other end.

USING FILIGREE CONNECTORS GIVES YOU LOTS OF HOLES AT DIFFERENT HEIGHTS AND PLACES SO THAT YOU CAN EASILY LINK THINGS TOGETHER.

- - - - - - -

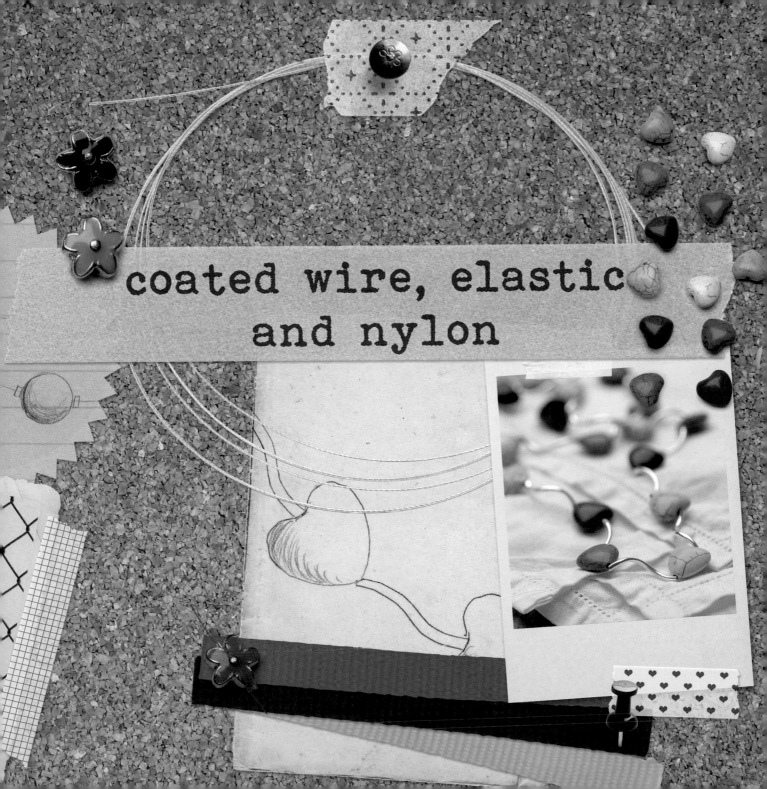

coated wire, elastic
and nylon

twists

The silver twisted tube
spacer beads create a
real sense of movement
in this simple design.

Everything you will need...

Using multi-strand elastic is a very simple way of stringing beads together without having to use any findings at all – and it doesn't matter how big or small you make the necklace, as you will be able to stretch it over your head!

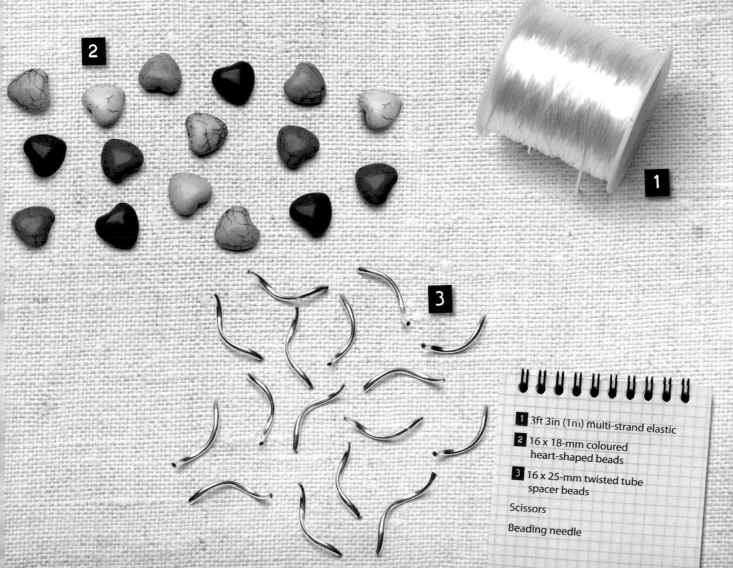

1 3ft 3in (1m) multi-strand elastic

2 16 x 18-mm coloured heart-shaped beads

3 16 x 25-mm twisted tube spacer beads

Scissors

Beading needle

twists

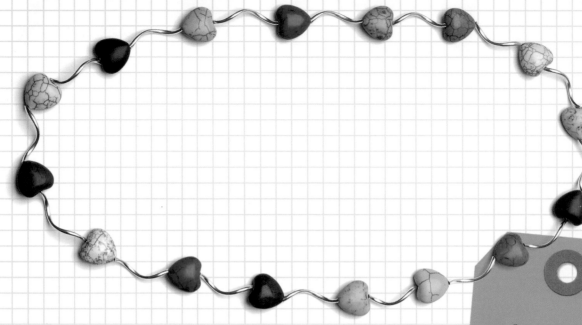

Assembling twists

1 Arrange the coloured heart-shaped beads, making sure that no two of the same colour are next to each other.

2 Thread your length of multi-strand elastic through the eye of the beading needle.

3 Thread on the first coloured heart-shaped bead, followed by a twisted tube spacer bead.

4 Repeat step 3, but this time thread the heart bead on upside down. Keep alternating heart beads and twisted tube spacer beads, and also the way the heart beads face, until you have used up all the beads.

5 Tie the two ends of the elastic in a knot, pulling the elastic tightly so that all the beads sit flush against each other.

6 Keeping the beading needle on one end of the elastic, thread it back through a few of the beads, so that the end is no longer near the tied knot. Cut off any excess. Thread the beading needle onto the other end of the elastic and repeat this process, going the other way around the necklace.

IF YOU ARE USING HEAVIER BEADS SUCH AS CERAMIC OR METAL, TRY TO KEEP THE NECKLACE SHORT SO THAT THE ELASTIC DOESN'T STRETCH UNDER THE WEIGHT.

STRINGING BEADS UPRIGHT AND THEN UPSIDE
DOWN, LIKE THE HEART BEADS IN THIS
PROJECT, MEANS THERE IS NO RIGHT OR WRONG
WAY TO THE NECKLACE. IT DOESN'T MATTER
WHICH WAY ROUND IT IS WORN.

illusion

Nylon wire is so fine that
you can create the illusion
that beads are floating
around your neck.

Everything you will need...

The crimps in this project are used as stoppers for the beads rather than being fully crimped.

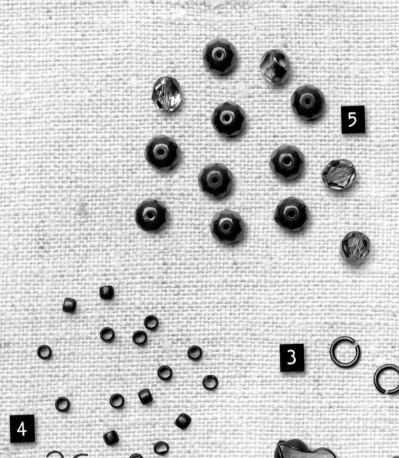

1 3 x 20-in (500mm) lengths of $^1/_{64}$in (0.3mm) nylon

2 2 x $^1/_8$-in (3mm) copper calottes

3 2 x $^1/_8$-in (4mm) copper jump rings

4 26 x $^1/_{16}$-in (1mm) copper crimp tubes

5 13 x 8-mm beads

6 1 x $^1/_2$-in (12mm) copper lobster clasp

Side or top cutters

Flat-nose pliers

Round-nose pliers

Snipe-nose pliers

Ruler

x26

Assembling illusion

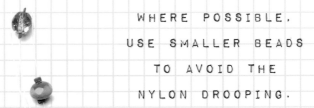

1 Cut 3 x 20-in (50cm) lengths of nylon and, holding all the ends together, thread them through the hole on a small calotte. Tie a knot as near to the end of the threads as possible.

2 Slide the calotte along the nylon with your fingers to cover the knot. Using flat-nose pliers, gently squash the two hemispheres together to close the calotte over the knot.

3 Cut off the excess nylon ends and close the calotte's 'tail' with round-nose pliers, forming a small eye loop. Link a 1/8-in (4mm) jump ring through this eye loop and close.

4 Now that you have made one end of the necklace, you have a more accurate guide to measuring your nylon strands to 16in (40cm) long. Place the strands along a ruler and, starting 2 1/2 in (6cm) from the calotte, mark dots every 2 1/2 in (6cm) on strand 1 and strand 3 using a pen. Then mark strand 2, starting 3 1/2 in (9cm) from the calotte and marking every 2 1/2 in (6cm), so that the marks are evenly staggered along the necklace length. Do this for a total of 13 1/2 in (34cm), so that you end up with another gap of 2 1/2 in (6cm) where you will add the calotte at the other end of the necklace.

WHERE POSSIBLE,
USE SMALLER BEADS
TO AVOID THE
NYLON DROOPING.

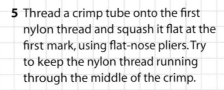

5 Thread a crimp tube onto the first nylon thread and squash it flat at the first mark, using flat-nose pliers. Try to keep the nylon thread running through the middle of the crimp.

6 Slide your first bead followed by another crimp tube onto the nylon, so that they sit flush against the first crimp. Squash the crimp tube tightly onto the nylon to secure the bead in place.

7 Repeat steps 5 and 6 until all the beads and crimps are secured on the nylon strands.

8 Repeat steps 1 and 2, adding a calotte to the other end of the necklace. Cut off any excess nylon ends.

9 Using round-nose pliers, close the calotte's 'tail' to form an eye loop. Link a lobster clasp onto a 1/8-in (4mm) jump ring, link the jump ring through the calotte eye loop and close.

THIS NECKLACE WORKS BEST AT A SHORT LENGTH OF ABOUT 16IN (40CM).

illusion

weaver

This is a very elegant necklace:
the wire is woven through alternate
beads, creating a rhythmical pattern.

Everything you will need...

You can be as colourful as you like with your choice of beads, or use beads that are all from the same colour palette, as I have done.

1. 3ft 3in (1m) nylon-coated wire
2. 2 x $\frac{1}{16}$-in (2mm) crimp tubes
3. 2 x purple $\frac{1}{4}$-in (7mm) jump rings
4. 2 x $\frac{1}{8}$-in (3mm) crimp covers
5. 27 x 8-mm cut-glass beads
6. 1 x $\frac{1}{2}$-in (12mm) purple lobster clasp

Side or top cutters

Crimping pliers

Snipe-nose pliers

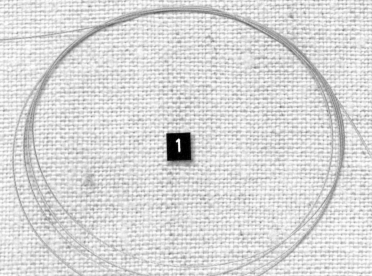

Assembling weaver

1 Cut the nylon-coated wire in half and thread both pieces through a crimp tube, keeping the tube approximately 2in (5cm) from one end.

2 Thread both ends of the wire through a jump ring and back through the crimp tube. Slide the crimp tube towards the jump ring, so that it just touches the jump ring.

3 Using crimping pliers, squash the crimp tube and then add a crimp cover to conceal it. Cut away any excess wire.

4 Thread both ends of the wire through one bead, then separate the wires and add another bead onto one wire only.

5 Thread both wires through another bead, then separate the wires again. This time, add a bead to the single wire not used in step 4.

6 Continue adding beads in this way, alternating the wires, until you have used all 27 beads.

7 Thread another crimp tube onto both wires directly after the last bead, then thread both ends of the wire through a jump ring and back through the crimp tube. Using crimping pliers, squash the tube and add another crimp cover over the top.

8 Finally, re-open one of the jump rings at one end, link on the lobster clasp and close the jump ring.

THE SIMPLICITY OF THIS NECKLACE MEANS THAT THE BEAUTY OF THE BEADS AND FINDINGS REALLY STANDS OUT.

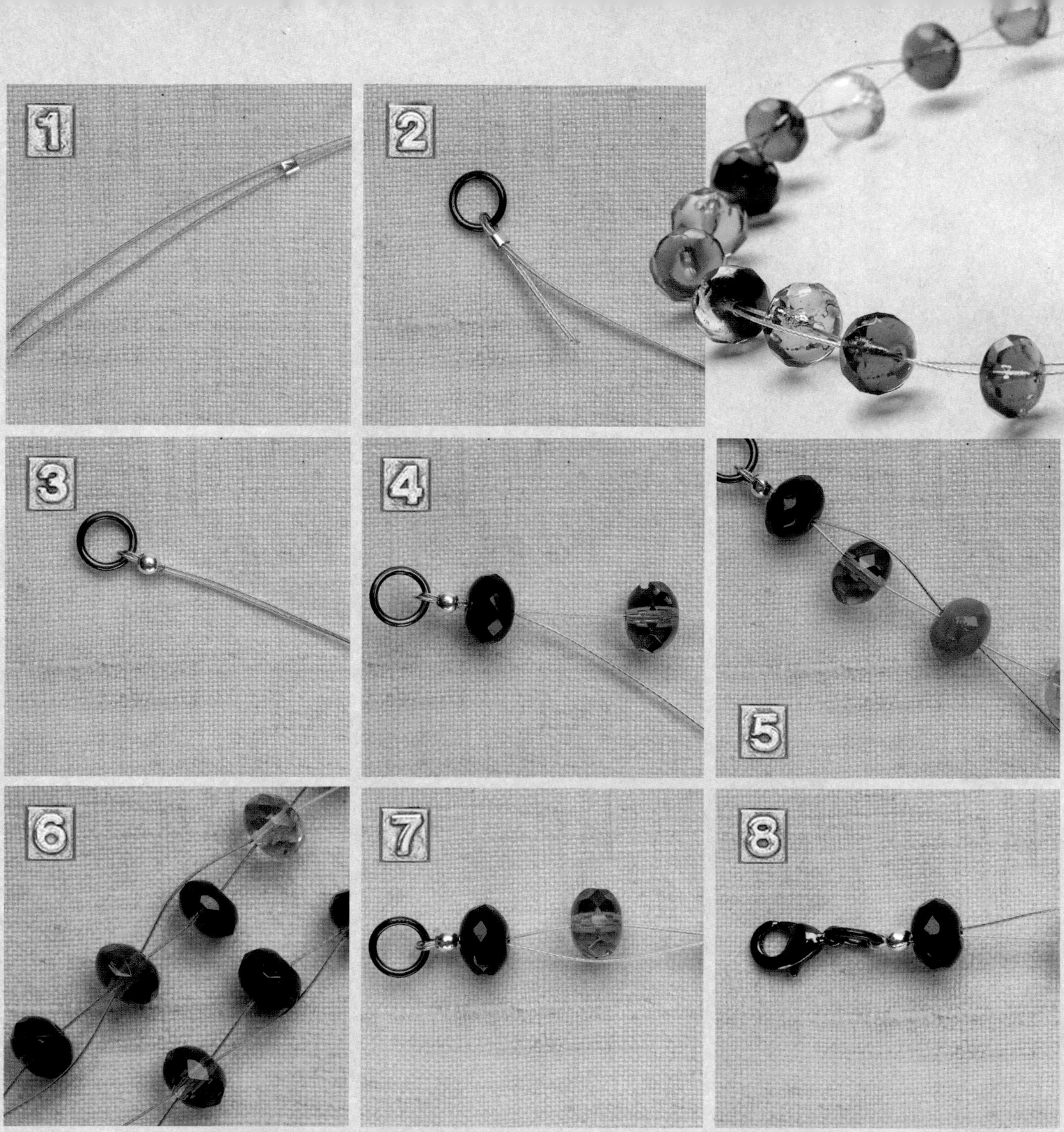
1
2
3
4
5
6
7
8

criss-
cross

This design shows off
the range of patterns
you can create with
just crimps and
nylon-coated wire.

Everything you will need...

This project uses most of the crimps as stoppers for the beads, in the same way as in the Illusion project on page 88.

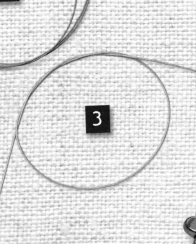

8 18 x 5-mm fluted beads

9 2 x 14-mm blue daisy beads

10 2 x 14-mm yellow daisy beads

11 2 x 14-mm pink daisy beads

Side or top cutters

Crimping pliers

Flat-nose pliers

Ruler

1 40-in (1m) blue nylon-coated wire

2 40-in (1m) pink nylon-coated wire

3 40-in (1m) yellow nylon-coated wire

4 2 x 1/2-in (12mm) bead cones

5 41 x 1/16 x 1/16-in (1 x 1mm) crimp tubes

6 2 x 5/8-in (15mm) three-holed separators

7 1 x 3/4-in (20mm) round magnetic clasp

criss-cross

Assembling criss-cross

1 Cut the three lengths of coloured nylon-coated wire in half and group them so that you have 2 x 20-in (50cm) groups, each containing one strand of each colour. Pass one group through 1 x bead cone, 1 x crimp tube, through the loop on one half of a magnetic clasp and back through the crimp tube.

2 Slide the crimp tube up the wire threads so that it just touches the magnetic clasp and squash it using crimping pliers. Cut off any excess wires. Slide the bead cone over the crimp tube to conceal it. You may need to pinch the top of the cone to secure it in place. Repeat steps 1 and 2 for the other group of coloured wires.

3 Starting with the group of wires to the left of the magnetic clasp, keep all the wires taut and measure 4¹/₂in (11.5cm) along the wires from the bottom of the bead cone, making a mark on each strand with a pen. Slide 1 x crimp tube onto each wire and squash in place at the marked point, using flat-nose pliers. Then add 1 x gold fluted bead, 1 x three-holed separator, 1 x gold fluted bead and 1 x crimp tube to each wire. Push all the beads up snugly against each other and crimp the last crimp tube, using flat-nose pliers to secure the cluster together. Repeat this step for the group of wires on the right-hand side of the clasp.

4 Measure 1¹/₂in (4cm) along both of the blue wires and make a mark with a pen. Add 1 x crimp tube to each wire and crimp at the marked point with a pair of flat-nose pliers. Then add 1 x blue daisy bead and 1 x crimp tube to each wire. Crimp the last crimp tube with flat-nose pliers to secure the daisy bead in place.

5 Next, measure 1³/₄in (4.5cm) along each yellow wire and repeat step 4, using a yellow daisy bead. Then measure 2in (5cm) along each pink wire and repeat, using a pink daisy bead.

6 Take the two blue wires and thread them both through a crimp tube. Next, manipulate the wires so that they cross over one another. When you are happy with the positioning of the crimp tube, squash it flat with flat-nose pliers.

7 Take the middle yellow wire on one side, thread on another crimp tube and pass one of the blue wires through the same crimp tube. When you are happy with the position, squash the crimp tube flat using flat-nose pliers. Repeat for the other side. You must try to squash the crimp tube at the same point on both sides, keeping the design symmetrical. Repeat using the pink wires and blue wires.

8 Continue adding crimp tubes and squashing them in place, so that the wires form a criss-cross diamond pattern in the middle.

9 Finally, add a fluted bead and crimp tube to each wire. Squash the tube at the ends of the wire to prevent the bead from falling off.

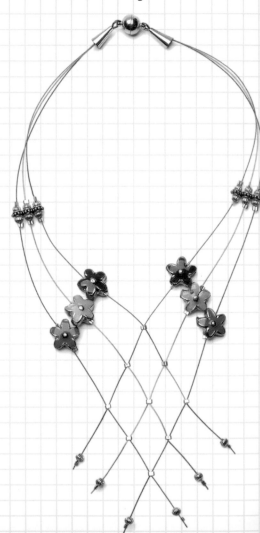

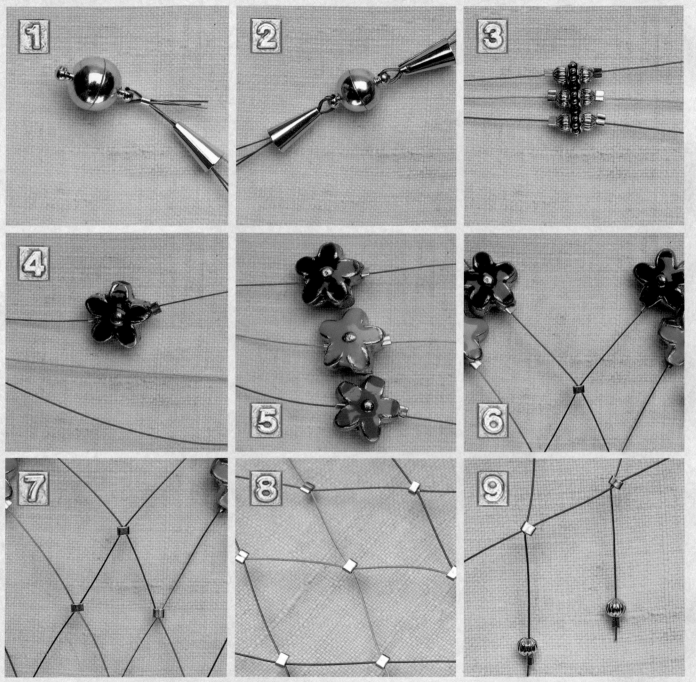

AVOID USING HEAVY BEADS - IT CAN DISTORT THE SHAPE OF THE NYLON.

recycled
objects

vintage

My passion for buttons keeps
growing, especially when I came
across these beautiful vintage
cut-glass and crystal buttons.

Everything you will need...

The best buttons to use have two or four holes all the way through them, rather than a shaft at the back with the hole going through it. The great thing about this technique is that it suits brightly coloured modern buttons, too!

1 5-ft (1.5m) ¹/₁₆-in (1mm) clear elastic

2 Approximately 30 x crystal or glass buttons, 10–25mm in size

3 2 x ⁵/₁₆-in (8mm) chain ends

4 2 x ¹/₈-in (4mm) jump rings

5 1 x ¹/₄-in (6mm) bolt ring

Scissors

Crimping pliers

Snipe-nose pliers

vintage

Assembling vintage

1 Cut 1 x 20-in (50cm), 1 x 18-in (45cm) and 1 x 16-in (40cm) lengths of ¹/₁₆-in (1mm) elastic and lay out your buttons in three rows. Ensure that each row has the largest buttons in the middle and the smallest ones at either end. Use at least ten buttons on each strand of elastic.

2 Start threading your buttons onto each elastic length, pushing the elastic down through the left-hand hole on the button and up through the right-hand hole on the same button. If the button has four holes, use two holes that are diagonally opposite each other.

3 Continue adding buttons to all three lengths of elastic. It's easy to move the buttons by just lifting the elastic between the holes.

4 Gather the three lengths of elastic so that all the ends are at the same point and thread them through a chain end so that they poke out the other end.

5 Using crimping pliers, crimp the middle of the chain end so that it squashes all the elastic threads, holding them in place. Cut off the excess elastic that was sticking out the other end. Repeat steps 5 and 6 to secure the other side of the necklace in the other chain end.

6 Open a jump ring and link the bolt ring to it, then link the jump ring onto the loop of one chain end and close. Open another jump ring, link it to the loop on the other chain end and close.

LAYER BUTTONS
ON TOP OF
EACH OTHER TO
ADD AN EXTRA
DIMENSION TO
YOUR DESIGN.

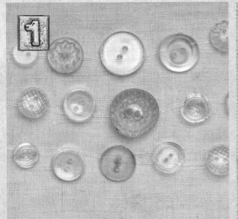

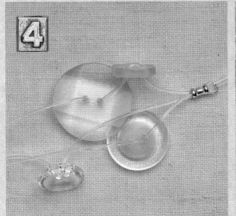

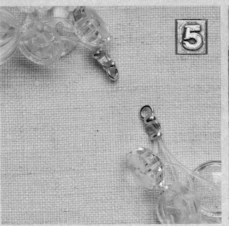

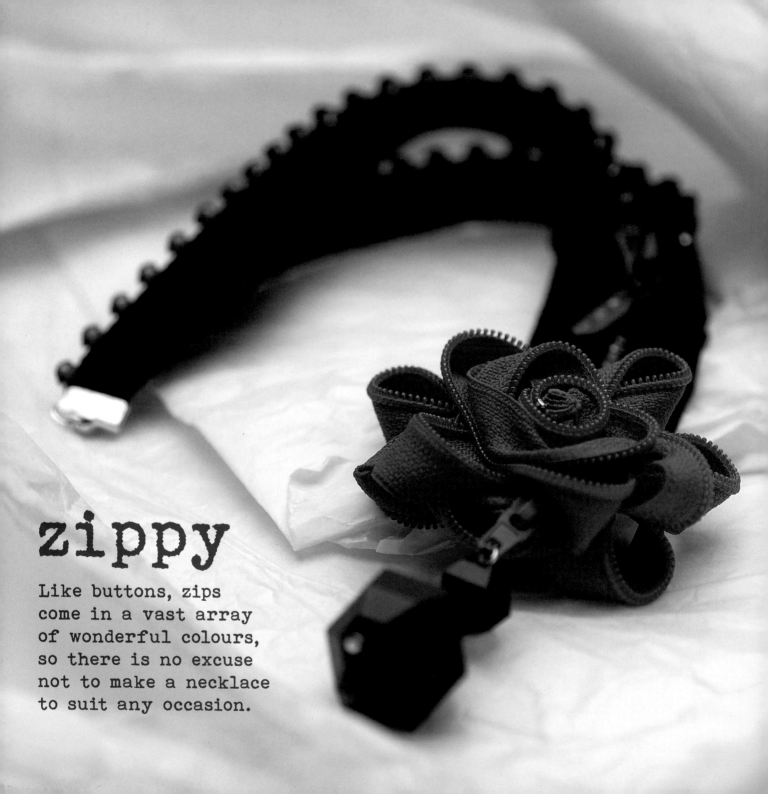

zippy

Like buttons, zips
come in a vast array
of wonderful colours,
so there is no excuse
not to make a necklace
to suit any occasion.

Everything you will need...

The length of your zip will determine the size of the rose.

1. 1 x 20-in (500mm) pink zip
2. 1 x 12-in (300mm) black diamante zip
3. 2 x ⁵⁄₈-in (15mm) ribbon crimps
4. 2 x ¹⁄₈-in (4mm) jump ring
5. 1 x ¹⁄₂-in (12mm) lobster clasp
6. 1 x ¹⁄₄-in (7mm) jump ring
7. 1 x 2-in (50mm) head pin
8. 1 x 25-mm faceted black bead
9. 1 x 2-in (50mm) eye pin
10. 1 x 15-mm faceted black bead

Dressmaking needle

Pink cotton thread

Scissors

Flat-nose pliers

Snipe-nose pliers

Round-nose pliers

Side or top cutters

Assembling zippy

1 Unzip the 20-in (500mm) pink dress zip as far as it will go, so that the zip is still joined but you have two separate halves to work with. Starting from one of the ends without the zip pull attached, form a tight spiral of a couple of turns. Using a dressmaking needle and matching pink thread, hand sew a couple of stitches to secure the spiral.

2 Form a small section of the zip into a loop directly next to the stitched spiral, then hand stitch the loop to the spiral.

3 Continue to form loops that overlap each other like the petals of a rose. The loops will naturally become larger as you move around the spiral. Remember to sew a stitch or two at each loop to hold them all in place.

4 When you get to the bottom of the zip, make sure that the zip pull is hanging down and doesn't get caught up in a loop and stitched. Now take the second half of the zip and start to form more loops, continuing around the ones made in steps 2 and 3, again adding a stitch or two as you go.

5 Keeping the black diamante dress zip closed, fold the bottom ends in to form a small triangular point. Stitch the zip right side down to the back of the rose, so that the pink zip pull is dangling down vertically and the diamantes of the black zip will be facing vertically when viewed from the front.

6 Unzip the black zip, so that you have two separate sections. Add a ribbon crimp to each end by sandwiching the zip ends between the ribbon crimp and squashing the crimp with flat-nose pliers.

7 Open 1 x ⅛-in (4mm) jump ring and link on the lobster clasp, then link the jump ring to one ribbon crimp end and close. Open the other ⅛-in (4mm) jump ring and add 1 x ¼-in (7mm) jump ring for the 'eye' of the clasp; link the ⅛-in (4mm) jump ring to the other end of the ribbon crimp and close.

8 Thread a head pin through the 25-mm black bead and form a closed eye loop as close to the top of the bead as possible. If the hole of your bead is too big, add a smaller bead first to trap the head pin.

9 Pass the eye pin through the smaller black bead and form an eye loop as close to the top of the bead as possible. Join the two beads together by the eye loops and finally link them onto the pink zip pull.

MAKE SURE YOU STITCH AT EVERY PETAL SO THAT THE ZIP ROSE DOESN'T UNRAVEL.

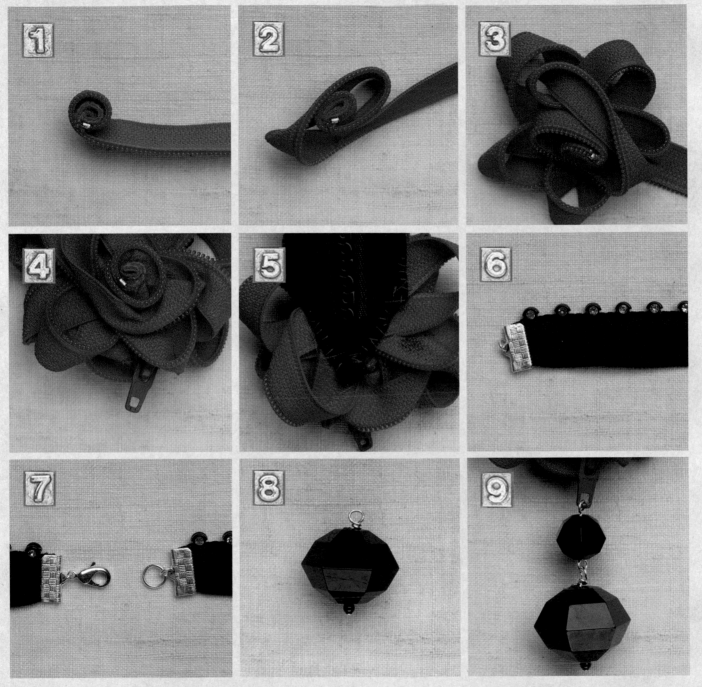

circles

Washing powder and fabric softeners come in lovely bright plastic containers that are the perfect material to form funky shapes for pendants.

Everything you will need...

Nylon-coated chokers come in a variety of colours, so will carry on the bright, funky theme of the plastic circles.

2

3

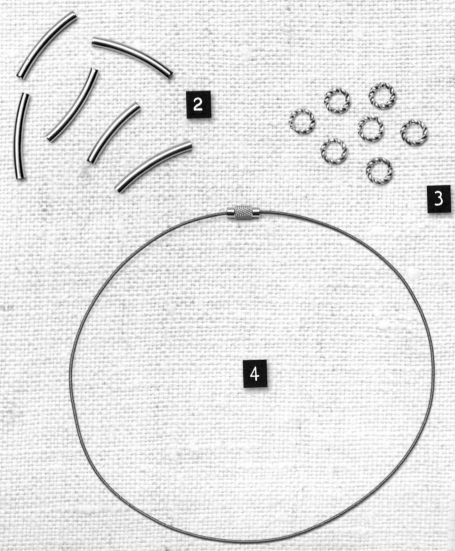

4

1

1. Assorted brightly coloured plastic containers

2. 6 x 35-mm curved tube spacers

3. 7 x ¼-in (6mm) twisted jump rings

4. 1 x 16-in (400mm) coloured plastic-coated wire choker with a screw end

Sharp scissors or circular cutters 1³⁄₈ in, 1in and ⁵⁄₈in (35mm, 25mm and 15mm) in diameter

Hand drill and 2mm drill bit (or bradawl)

Flat-nose pliers

circles

Assembling circles

1 Wash out a selection of brightly coloured plastic containers and soak off all labels. Locate the flattest area on the container and cut out that area with sharp scissors, so that you are left with flat, coloured pieces of plastic.

2 Ideally using stamps or cutters, cut out 7 x 1³/₈-in (35mm) circles, 7 x 1-in (25mm) circles and 7 x ¹/₂-in (15mm) circles. If you do not have cutters, use a compass, draw circles on the plastic and cut them out with sharp scissors.

3 Lay the circles on top of each other in order of size to make seven pendants of three different-coloured circles each.

4 Aligning the circles so that they all touch at the top, drill a small hole through them all using a hand drill and a 2mm drill bit. (Alternatively, lay the plastic on a cutting mat and, using a sharp bradawl, pierce through the plastic circles, making sure you keep the point away from your fingers at all times.) Open a twisted jump ring, thread on all three circles and link the jump ring onto the plastic-coated choker and close.

5 Unscrew the end of the wire choker and thread on a tube spacer.

6 Continue linking groups of circles onto the nylon choker by using the twisted jump rings and tube spacers until you have used up all the elements.

CUT DIFFERENT
SIZES SO THAT
YOU CAN LAYER
COLOURS ON TOP
OF EACH OTHER.

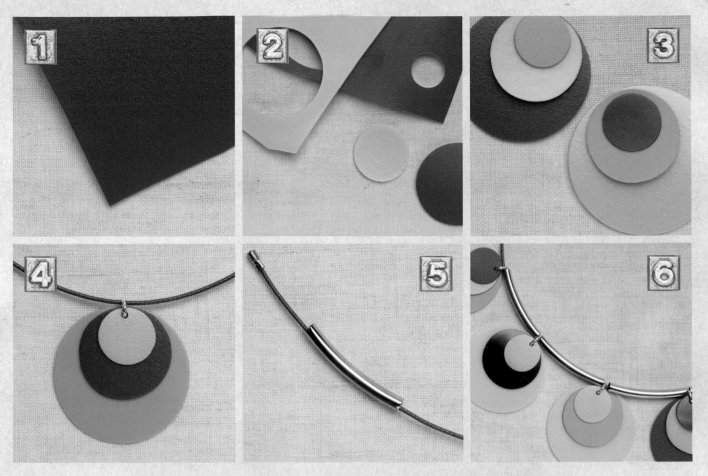

IF YOU CAN USE CUTTERS OR STAMPS TO CUT
OUT YOUR SHAPES, THE END RESULT CAN LOOK
MORE PROFESSIONAL - BUT SHARP SCISSORS
WORK JUST AS WELL IF YOU CUT CAREFULLY.

rocker

The safety pin is iconic to the punk era of the 1970s and 80s. This project gives it a modern, sparkling twist.

Everything you will need...

Safety pins are a good object to experiment with as they come in so many colours, styles and sizes.

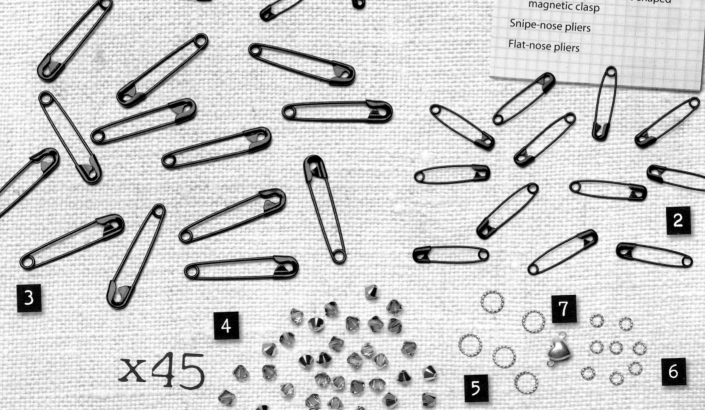

1. 12 x ³⁄₄-in (19mm) small safety pins
2. 12 x ⁷⁄₈-in (23mm) medium safety pins
3. 13 x 1¹⁄₄-in (30mm) large safety pins
4. 45 x 6-mm bicone crystals
5. 5 x ³⁄₈-in (10mm) twisted jump rings
6. 8 x ¹⁄₄-in (6mm) twisted jump rings
7. 1 x ⁵⁄₈-in (16mm) heart-shaped magnetic clasp

Snipe-nose pliers

Flat-nose pliers

x45

USING SILVER
TWISTED JUMP RINGS
AMONG THE BLACK PINS
CREATES A STRONG
CONTRAST AND
SPARKLING DETAIL.

Assembling rocker

1 Place your safety pins in order of size, so that you have 1 x large pin in the middle with 1 x medium-sized and 1 x small pin on either side of it.

2 Open all the safety pins. Slide 3 x 6-mm crystals onto the large pin, 2 x 6-mm crystals onto both of the medium-sized pins and 1 x 6-mm crystal onto both of the small pins.

3 Keeping all the safety pins with the 'tails' at the top, link them in height order onto 1 x $^3/_8$-in (10mm) twisted jump ring. Before closing the jump ring, add a further large pin on either side of your group of five pins. Close the jump ring.

4 Repeat steps 1 to 3, this time linking the large pin added at the end of step 3 to the second twisted jump ring, so that the two clusters of pins and crystals are joined together.

5 Repeat step 4 so that you have five clusters of safety pins joined together.

6 Take 1 x $^1/_4$-in (6mm) twisted jump ring and link it through the head of the large pin at the end of one cluster and through the tail of another large pin and close. Repeat for the other side.

7 Repeat step 6, using a medium-sized pin and then a small pin.

8 Finally, attach a heart-shaped magnetic clasp to each end of the necklace using a $^1/_4$-in (6mm) jump ring.

YOU CAN CHOOSE ANY
COLOUR OF CRYSTALS
FOR THIS PROJECT.

rocker

resources

SOURCES OF MATERIALS

UK

Angelas Jewellery Findings House
www.orangiboon-jewellery.vpweb.co.uk

Beadsunlimited
PO Box 1
Hove
East Sussex BN3 3SG
Tel: +44 (0)1273 740777
www.beadsunlimited.co.uk

Bead Aura
3 Neals Yard
Covent Garden
London WC2H 9DP
Tel: +44 (0)20 7836 3002
www.beadaura.co.uk

Beadworks UK Ltd
Trading as The Bead Shop
21a Tower Street
Covent Garden
London WC2H 9NS
Tel: +44 (0)20 7240 0931
www.beadshop.co.uk

Bijoux Beads
2 Abbey Street
Bath BA1 1NN
Tel: +44 (0)1225 482024
www.bijouxbeads.co.uk

Chings Beads & Jewellery Ltd
www.beadsnjewellery.co.uk

Cookson Precious Metals Ltd
59–83 Vittoria Street
Birmingham B1 3NZ
Tel: +44 (0)845 100 1122
www.cooksongold.com

Jewellery Shed
www.jewelleryshed.co.uk

Oaks Jewellery Craft
www.oaksjewellerycraft.co.uk

Palmer Metals
401 Broad Lane
Coventry CV5 7AY
Tel: +44 (0)845 6449343
www.palmermetals.co.uk

Shiney Company
5 Saville Row
Bath BA1 2QP
Tel: +44 (0)1225 332 506
www.shineyrocks.co.uk

Spoilt Rotten Beads
7 The Green
Haddenham
Ely
Cambridgeshire CB6 3TA
Tel: +44 (0)1353 749853
www.spoiltrottenbeads.co.uk

The Bead Shop Scotland
29 Court Street
Haddington
East Lothian EH14 3AE
Tel: +44 (0)1620 822886
www.beadshopscotland.co.uk

WORLDWIDE
Beadaholique
www.beadaholique.com

Cortes de Perles
www.yosbeads.com

Sunshine Discount Crafts
www.sunshinecrafts.com

BOOKS
500 Necklaces: Contemporary Interpretations of a Timeless Form
Marthe Le Van (Lark Books, 2007)

A World of Necklaces
Anne Leurquin and Mauro Magliani
(Skira Editore, 2003)

acknowledgments

I would like to say thank you to Rosie Wheeler for her brilliant ideas and to Emma Duke and Claire Rockett for their endless entertainment when we work together at shows. Finally, I would like to say thank you to all the staff at GMC Publications for giving me this opportunity to write my second book.

about the author

Tansy Wilson graduated from Brighton University in the south-east of England with a BA Honours Degree in Three-dimensional Design. She also obtained a Post Graduate Certificate in Education. In addition to being a part-time lecturer, she currently works for the University of the Arts London as an External Moderator for Foundation Art and Design programmes as well as Drawing Awards and Certificates. Tansy has her own business making bespoke jewellery for private clients and produces a craft range to sell at shows. She also writes articles and creates projects for *Making Jewellery* and *Making* magazines.

index

To place an order, or request
a catalogue, contact:

GMC Publications Ltd
Castle Place, 166 High Street,
Lewes, East Sussex, BN7 1XU
United Kingdom

Tel: +44 (0)1273 488005
Fax: +44 (0)1273 402866

www.gmcbooks.com